BIRMINGHAM AT WAR VOL 2

ALTON DOUGLAS
CLIVE HARDY
GORDON STRETCH

ADDITIONAL RESEARCH BY JO DOUGLAS.

© 1987, Alton & Jo Douglas.
ISBN 0 9508455 4 X
Printed and Published by Streetly Printing (Birmingham) Ltd., 61 Curzon Street, Birmingham, B4 7XG.
2nd Impression January 1987.

CONTENTS

c/o The Birmingham Post & Mail Ltd.,
28 Colmore Circus,
Birmingham B4 6AX.

Dear Nostalgic,

Well, here I am just one year after our journey into the time frozen world of "Birmingham at War" was launched, excitedly involved with Volume Two. The reaction to the first book was, to risk a cliche, quite overwhelming, and my trunk of never-to-be-disposed-of items is now topped up with the most encouraging "thank you" letters from as close to home as Northfield and as far afield as Waikapura and Nova Scotia.

Incidentally, the attached photograph is in response to your query about MY activities during those troubled years. As you'll gather from this May 1940 snap, my "Birmingham at War" efforts were mainly concerned with the complicated business of growing up!

After we had completed the first book many other good photographs surfaced. People wrote, telephoned and even travelled, to let me know that they too had interesting material. Clive, Gordon, Jo and I then set about, a busy bunch of moles, unearthing more gems until the collection you see here gradually took on a life of its own. A great many of these items have never seen daylight before because they were either protected by the Official Secrets Act until recently, or, in some instances, due to the strict censorship laws of the time, quite frankly should never have been taken at all! In the latter case, we can only thank whichever God it is who looks after these things that they were, as they help to make documents of this nature quite unique.

We've included a few absorbing "I was there" anecdotes and have had to leave out even more. One unsubstantiated story tells of a pub in Aston on a Saturday night (piano playing, sing-song - typical hullabloo), the publican called "Time", went upstairs, opened his bedroom door and there lying on his bed was an unexploded bomb!

As far as the text is concerned, we've tried to avoid going over the same ground as the first book, but we felt that a few mental nudges (such as the origin of the Home Guard) would serve a useful purpose, without actually driving you into the arms of Morpheus. We've also discovered some more startlingly dramatic examples of bomb damage, the military's involvement and war production, and our new categories include animals at war, factory concerts, war brides, Brummies abroad, etc.

From a purely personal point of view, my involvement with these two books has made me wish I could climb to the top of the Town Hall, as Godfrey Baseley did so long ago. Once there, I'd proclaim to the world that I was proud to be A BRUMMIE.

Yours, in friendship,

Alton

About Alton Douglas

Alton Douglas is probably best known as the quizmaster (and co-writer) of the top-rated BBC TV series 'KNOW YOUR PLACE", but he is also a professional comedian, after-dinner speaker, TV and radio character actor, showbiz/jazz book and record reviewer, TV and radio commercial voice-over artist, ex-5th Royal Inniskilling Dragoon Guards trombonist, the voice behind several cartoons and children's toys, etc.

He has appeared in virtually every major theatre in the U.K. (including the London Palladium) and is the veteran of hundreds of television studio warm-ups, but these days specialises in good class hotel, restaurant, conference and theatre work, either as a sophisticated and highly original comic or as an after-dinner speaker.

Currently his Sunday peaktime programme on Beacon Radio is proving to be extremely popular.

He has been featured as an actor in the TV programmes "Angels", "Seconds Out", "Crossroads" and "A Soft Touch" and in 1982 appeared in a strong dramatic role as John Rutland in Central's "Muck and Brass". His other television appearances include "The Golden Shot" (which he hosted on one memorable occasion), "The Knockers", "The Original Alton Douglas", "Nights at the Swan" and "Watch this Space", etc.

Living in the delightful Birmingham suburb of Kings Norton with his wife Jo and Old English Sheepdog Groucho Max (after two of his idols, Marx and Wall), he is a keep-fit enthusiast whose main interests are cricket, jazz, reading biographies and showbiz in general. He describes himself as a workaholic who likes to be involved in every stage of any project.

As a writer he is already the co-author/compiler of several books. The first, based on his TV series and entitled "Alton Douglas's Know Your Place", was published in 1981, followed by "Birmingham at War", which was an even greater success, selling over 10,000 copies within a few weeks of its launching in November, 1982. November, 1983 sees the publication of "Birmingham at War Vol ll" and "Coventry at War", and in May, 1984 "Joe Russell's Smethwick" will appear.

THE PRE-WAR SCENE

It was the Kondor Legion, a Luftwaffe force operating with Franco's Nationalists during the Spanish Civil War, which effectively demonstrated the use of air power to the rest of Europe. The most famous incident occurred on 27th april 1937, when the Spanish city of Guernica was attacked by German aircraft. Though a considerable amount of damage was done, rumour, hysterical reporting and propaganda distorted the event so much that many believed that the city had benn totally destroyed.

Our military thinkers agreed that in a future war our cities would be subjected to sudden and devasting attacks with HE bombs and gas, and that not only would there be crippling damage, but that the morale of the general public would collapse very quickly.

Since the mid-thirties there had been active discussion both in parliament and in public on what could be done to protect the civilian population in the event of war. The Air Raid Precautions Act of 1937 laid the foundations of our civil defence and was partially put to the test during the Czechoslovakian Crisis, when gas masks were issued, trench shelters dug in public parks, anti-aircraft guns we had were trundled into position, and tentative plans for the evacuation of children from our cities were drawn up. War seemed inevitable, but Neville Chamberlain gave way to Hitler's demands at Munich, thereby defusing the situation.

As rearmament got under way, the Royal Navy and the Royal Air Force were given priority, and it is interesting to note than on 22nd December 1937, Chamberlain's Cabinet overruled the nation's air experts and authorised that priority be given to the production of fighters rather than bombers. Had this action not been taken then the Battle of Britain might well have ended differently. Priority within the army was given to anti-aircraft guns, though in 1938 there were not enough of them available to equip some units with even a training piece, and our armoured formations were equipped with an odd assortment of tank prototypes whilst other forces were receiving quantity deliveries. In March, 1939 it was announced that the Territorial Army was to be expanded from 12 to 26 divisions which would fight alongside our 6 regular divisions. By comparison since 1934, the German Army had been expanded from 100,000 men to a force comprising 6 panzer and 10 motorised divisions and a further 88 divisions which, though dependent on horse transport, were equipped with modern weapons.

To many the declaration of war on Sunday 3rd September 1939 was a tremendous relief from the tension and uncertainty that had gripped Europe for several years. There was none of the cheering and dancing in the streets that had accompanied the declaration of war in August, 1914.

CHARLES SIMPSON:
"As a Birmingham councillor on the Airport Committee I was invited by the German Air Ministry to make a civic visit. Ironically this photograph shows myself (2nd hat carrier from the left) with pilots and officials, including several members of the Nazi Party, standing in front of the World War I Memorial in Berlin. A few months later we were involved in World War II."

4 *Hitler leads Neville Chamberlain into his mountain chalet at Berchtesgaden, 15th September 1938.*

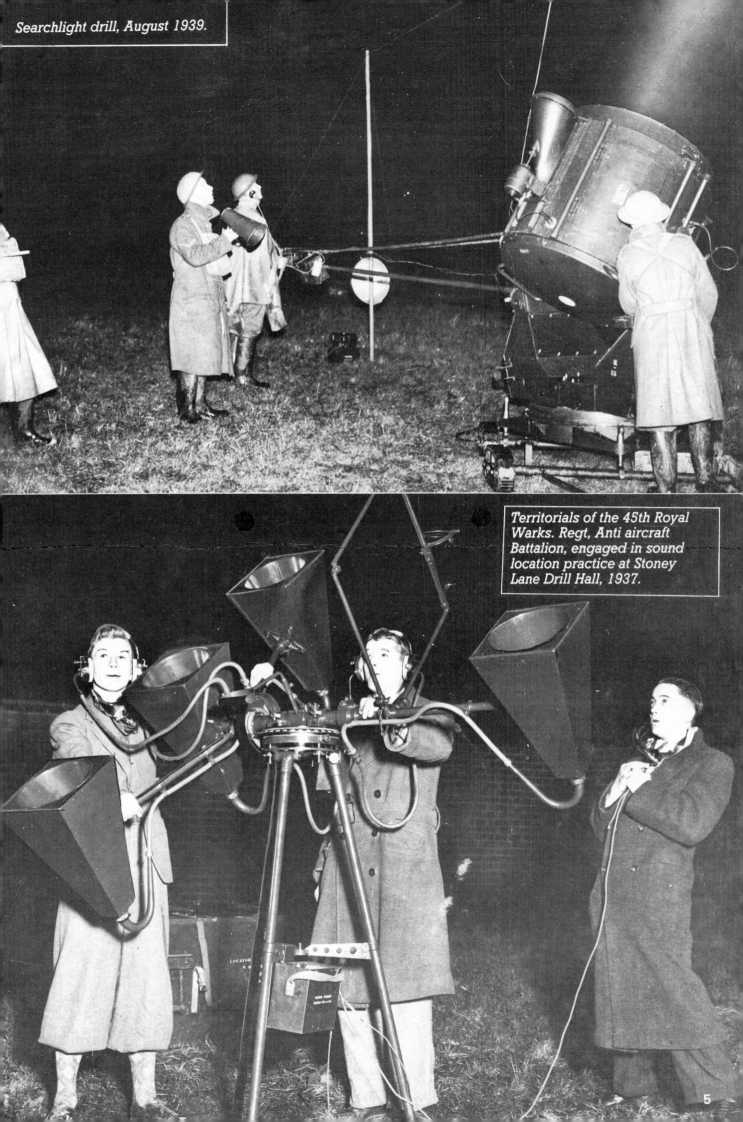

Searchlight drill, August 1939.

Territorials of the 45th Royal Warks. Regt, Anti aircraft Battalion, engaged in sound location practice at Stoney Lane Drill Hall, 1937.

5

Your A·B·C· of A·R·P·

Two lengths of wood and some screws will help to lighten 'gas mask' blues. Now it is an easy task to take out baby and his mask.

NEW A·R·P HELMET
QUICK ACTION
VISOR

PRICE 4/6

- Prevents splinter and blast injury to eyes and forehead.
- Gives greater confidence and enables user to have both hands free for the job.
- Ample vision through fine gauge mesh riveted into position, yet obviates blinding glare effect of the burning bombs.
- No rattle or working loose.
- Easily fitted into position and securely held by two screws.
- Will not jerk off; rim of helmet fits snugly into groove in visor.
- Instantly lifted up out of vision when not in use and held in place by spring tension and two small stops which locate on rim of helmet.

A.R.P. SHOULD stand for Arrangement, Resolve and Preparedness in household affairs

BISCUIT tins, with the lid and edges sealed with strong adhesive tape, are ideal for storing food

CHILDREN, restless in enforced inactivity between " Warning " and " All Clear " signals, can be amused by reading or telling them a story.

DARK blinds are difficult to fit quite accurately in many cases; overcome the difficulty by making a frame of plywood to fit the window, sticking black paper between it with drawing pins and a thin piece of wood across.

EAT good meals during the strain, and have a cup of hot milk or tea before going to bed, to induce drowsiness.

FIRST-AID equipment should be placed where all can get it easily, and should include good stores of anti-gas ointment, such as bleach powder or ointment, Elastoplast for cuts, iodine, bandages, pins, a small bottle of brandy and smelling salts.

GO to bed earlier and rise at an earlier hour these black-out days.

HELPFUL hints to remember during a raid should be pasted up on the door most used

IODINE application to yourself or others in a hurry may stain your frock. Dampen the stain, rub into it a quantity according to the stain, of bicarbonate of soda, leave for a day, wash, and if still slightly stained, have it cleaned.

JARS, screw-top, should be kept filled with barley sugar and raisins to nibble during a raid.

KNIT blankets, bed socks, mufflers, etc., from odd pieces of wool or old unpicked wool, which will unravel if washed in soapy lather or tightly wound round a hot water bottle.

LETTERS from home are going to be most eagerly sought by the men in the Services; make them gay, chatty, and give all the little details

MASKS may get damp, but don't dry them by artificial heat; put them out in a warm room to dry gradually, then get a waterproof cover as soon as possible for the container.

NATIONAL Service often means keeping on with the same job; it will hinder rather than help to neglect the home and those in it for an outside job

OINTMENT for gas casualties may get scarce, so buy your portion as soon as possible, but don't hoard selfishly. Get enough, but remember others !

PAILS of sand should be kept always filled with sand or earth to cover incendiary bombs.

QUIETNESS during the day is essential for night A.R.P. workers, so remember to keep the radio tuned down

READ something light during an air-raid ; try E. M. Delafield, P. G. Wodehouse, Beverley Nichols' garden books.

SMILES may seem secondary, but they, too, are a good defence.

TIMID folk probably can't help their terrors. If you know of any take them under your wing, invite them in during a raid if possible, and keeep them cheery.

USE as much available space as possible to grow veget-ables; ask your seedsman what seeds can be planted during the winter

VENTILATION (after using a gas-proof room for some hours) is important. Open the door wide

WARDENS' advice and requests should be obeyed instantly, personal feelings put aside and respect always given to men who are only doing their duty, however interfering it may seem.

XTRA courage is gained if you think of possible danger this way: " I've got to die sometime and if it is now that's just too bad, but why worry?

YOU can best serve by doing your job to the best of your ability at home, and leaving the war proper to politicians and the magnificent defence services.

ZENITH of war service lies in cheerfulness, adaptability, perseverance, determination. Make these your watchwords.

(Opposite page, top left)
Officials inspect the compressed air cylinders which operate the siren.

(Opposite page, top right)
The siren on the roof of the Council House used in May, 1939 for practising A.R.P. evacuation. Employess would take refuge on the basement. The Censor insisted the hands on the photograph should read "4.30" before he would allow the picture to appear in newspapers.

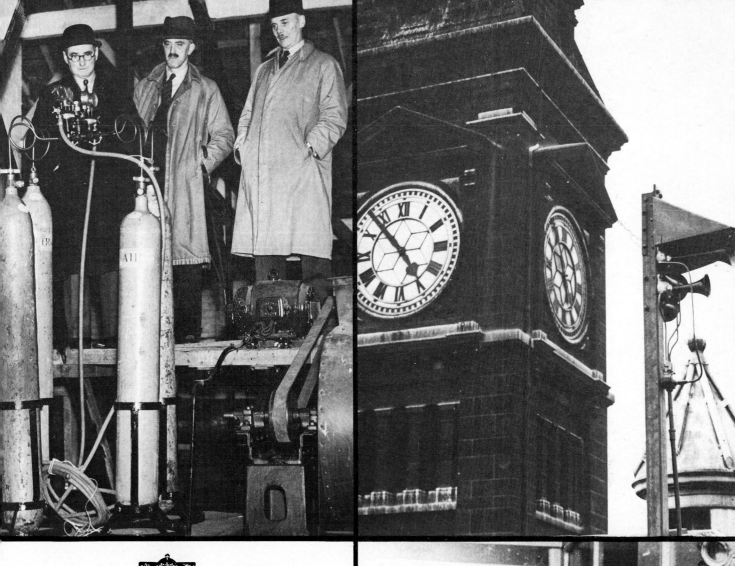

Issued by the Ministry of Home Security.

WHAT TO DO ABOUT GAS

OTHER COUNTRIES LOST THEIR FREEDOM in this war because they allowed the enemy to create confusion and panic among their civilian population so that the movement of defending armies was impeded.

We are not going to allow that to happen here. It won't happen if we are all on our guard, prepared to meet anything the enemy may do.

He may use gas. THE DANGER IS NOT SERIOUS if you do the right thing, both NOW and when the time comes. If you do, this weapon will have failed and you will have helped to beat it.

Here are the things to know and do. Read them carefully and remember them well in case the day comes. Keep this leaflet and look at it again.

HOW NOT TO GET GASSED.

NOW

1. In your gas mask you have the best possible protection against gases that affect your lungs or your eyes. It is a sure defence if you use it properly and in time. Make sure your own and your children's gas masks fit and are in working order : your warden or A.R.P. post can tell you. Practise putting them on and get used to wearing them with confidence. Your life may depend on whether you can put your mask on quickly. Remember to take off your spectacles before putting on your gas mask.

2. CARRY YOUR GAS MASK ALWAYS, and have it handy at night.

3. To prevent the face-piece misting over, smear a little soap lightly on the inside once a week.

4. If your chemist has " No. 2 Anti-gas ointment " (price 6d.) in stock, buy a jar. Read the instructions on the jar and carry it always. This ointment is for use as a protection against the effects of liquid blister gas.

IF THE GAS RATTLES SOUND.

1. PUT ON YOUR GAS MASK AT ONCE, wherever you are, even in bed.
2. TAKE COVER. Get into any nearby building as soon as you hear the rattle. Go upstairs if the building is a tall one. Close all windows in your house.

Don't come out or take your gas mask off till you hear the handbells ringing the " Gas clear ".

NEVER LOOK UPWARDS—you may get a drop of liquid gas in your eyes.

COVER YOUR SKIN UP so long as you are out of doors—hands in pockets, collar turned up. Or if you have an umbrella, put it up.

IF YOU DO GET GASSED.

GAS OR VAPOUR. If you breathe any gas or vapour—

1. PUT ON YOUR GAS MASK AT ONCE.

2. KEEP YOUR MASK ON, even though you may still feel some discomfort.

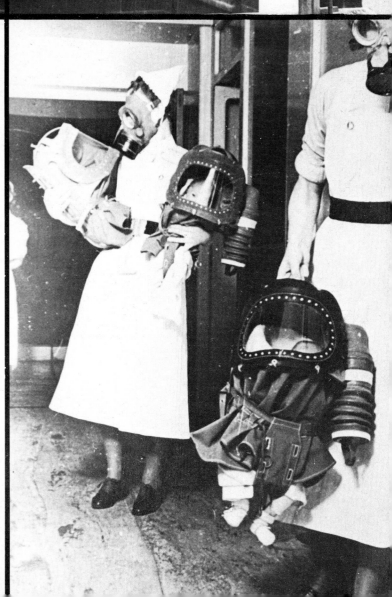

1—Shoring up an A.R.P. shelter after "damage" by a "high explosive bomb"
2—Removing an "incendiary bomb"
3—Decontaminating walls of the factory by means of bleach spraying
4—Demonstrating the use of foam appliances on oil and petrol fires
5—Washing down the factory walls by means of trailer pump to counteract the effects of persistent "gas bombs." This apparatus is used in conjunction with the trailer pump

6—The effect of a "high explosive bomb" in one of the workshops
7—Confining the effects of an "incendiary bomb" prior to removal
8—The General Office of the Personnel Block was turned into a temporary hospital
9—"Incendiary bomb" bursting in a wooden hut

10—Demonstrating the use of self-contained apparatus for rescuing "casualties" from an atmosphere charged with carbon monoxide gas. Note the life line

11—Rescuing a "casualty" from a wrecked surface trench. This was a demonstration in which all the A.R.P. personnel took part

12—Members of a First Aid Squad attending to a "casualty"

13—Members of a First Aid Squad attending to a "casualty" in the Medical Block

14—A Wreckage Squad leaving for the scene of action

15—A Wreckage Squad at the scene of action

16—A general view of operations showing an area which has been bleached by the Decontamination Squads

Children of St. Benedict's Road School, Small Heath, listen to instructions from the head master during their evacuation rehearsal this morning. *'B.Mail' 26/8/39*

BIRMINGHAM EVACUATION AREA

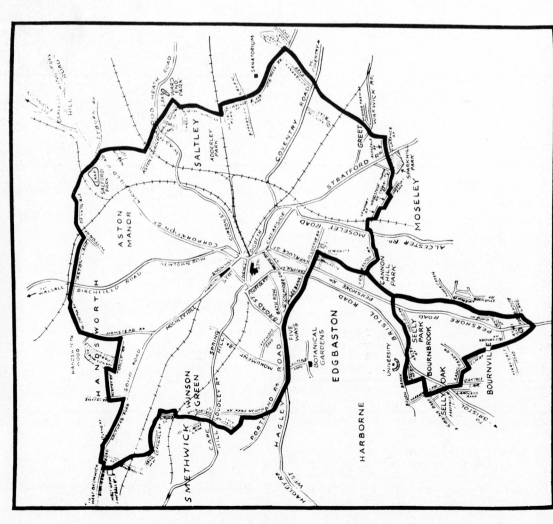

The dark line shown on this plan, as enclosing the central part of Birmingham with the additional triangular patch in the Selly Park area, marks the area from which children are to be evacuated. In fact the area does not end at the Smethwick boundary, but will be continued so as to enclose the densely populated parts of that town. *'B.Mail' 31/8/39*

FOOD FACTS

BRIGHTER
BREAKFASTS

ELP TO START THE DAY RIGHT

IF the family's got out of bed on the wrong side, if war-
ne routine looms extra dull and dreary, see how quickly these
ighter breakfasts will brighten the outlook!

They're easily prepared, tempting to look at and good to
ste. What's even more important, they provide body-fuel to
ep you warm in treacherous weather, and added energy to
lp you tackle the day's work without flagging.

**REAKFAST FRY helps to
in out the bacon .**

Ingredients : 2 rashers of fat bacon,
ely chopped, 4 dried eggs (recon-
tuted), salt and pepper. *Method:*
t the bacon in a frying-pan with-
t fat, and cook lightly. Pour in the
asoned egg, and cook without stir-
g until set and brown underneath.
ll up or cut in pieces, and serve
once.

**SH FRITTERS
ake a pleasant change**

Ingredients : 4 oz.
f-raising flour, or 4
. plain flour and 2
el teaspoons baking
wder, 1 level tea-
oon salt, quarter level
spoon pepper, 2 to 3
ied eggs, DRY, 2 to 3
blespoons water, quarter pint
lk,★ 2 to 3 oz. flaked cooked fish,
level tablespoon chopped parsley,
: for frying. *Method :* Mix flour,
king powder, salt, pepper and egg.
ake to a thick batter with the water
d milk. Beat well. Add fish and
rsley. Drop spoonfuls into a little
t fat in a frying-pan and fry until
lden brown on both sides. Serve
once. This makes 8 fritters.

MORE MARMALADE !
From April 1st your Preserves Coupon
will be worth 2 lb. marmalade *or* 1 lb.
preserves other than marmalade, *or*
1 lb. sugar.

**BREAKFAST PANCAKES
A savoury way with
fat bacon**

Ingredients : 2 rashers of fat
bacon, 1 small onion or leek,
chopped, 1 tablespoon chopped
parsley. *Batter :* 4 oz. flour, 1
dried egg, DRY, salt, 2 level teaspoons baking powder, quarter
pint milk,★ or milk and water.
Method : Cut up bacon
into small pieces and
fry with the chopped
onion. Mix the flour,
egg, salt and baking
powder to a smooth
batter with the milk or
milk and water. Add
the bacon, onion and
parsley to this. Drop
spoonfuls into a little
hot fat in a frying-pan
and fry till golden brown on
both sides.

"EGGY BREAD" is popular
with children. Reconstitute
1 dried egg and season with
salt, pepper and a pinch of
mustard. Dip slices of bread in
the egg, and fry in smoking hot
fat till brown. Chopped fried
bacon, chopped cooked vegetables or baked beans can be
served hot with the slices.

INTS CHANGES, Period No. 10, April 1st to April 28th:
ISINS (Stoned or Unstoned). Reduced from 8 to 4 points per lb.
No Change in Coupon Values: A—1, B—2, C—3.

TEN TO THE KITCHEN FRONT, TUESDAY, WEDNESDAY, THURSDAY & FRIDAY at 8.15 a.m.

E MINISTRY OF FOOD, LONDON, W.I. FOOD FACTS No. 248

An ex-hotel chef, who, because of the strenuous times, found himself
anaging a factory canteen, is mentioned in a Wartime Social Survey
eport:-

*He despaired of Birmingham's taste in food. He had been all round the
orld, and catering in Birmingham was the worst in the world. He said the
orkers at the factory only wanted fish and chips, cream cakes, bread and
tter, and brown gravy over everything. They had protested when he had
ade white sauce with boiled beef and carrots. They would not eat salads,
d not like savouries - 'Birmingham people do not understand food.'"*

HOME FRONT

The British Legion Canteen, 3rd December 1940.

W.V.S. canteen on a municipal car park.

FOOD FACTS

What's for "AFTERS"?

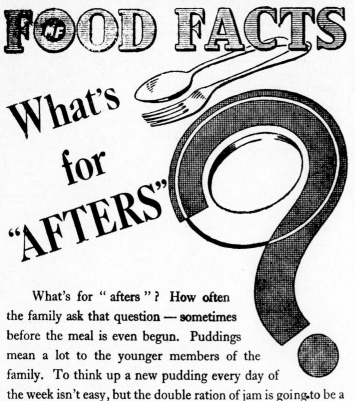

What's for "afters"? How often the family ask that question — sometimes before the meal is even begun. Puddings mean a lot to the younger members of the family. To think up a new pudding every day of the week isn't easy, but the double ration of jam is going to be a big help. What could be nicer or more nourishing than a steamed pudding dripping with plum jam, a jam omelette, or a plate of plain boiled rice served with a big spoonful of peach jam and the top of the milk? Other ideas for jam puddings are given below.

STEAMED FRUIT PUDDING

Ingredients: 8 oz. flour, 2 oz. fat, pinch of salt, 2 level teaspoons baking powder, water to mix, 1 lb. rhubarb or other fruit, 3 level tablespoonfuls jam. *Quantity*: 4 helpings. *Method*: Rub fat into the flour mixed with salt and baking powder. Add enough water to mix to a stiff dough. Roll out ¾ of this and line a greased basin with it. Put half the prepared fruit in the basin; then half the jam, the remaining fruit, and then the rest of the jam. Roll out the remaining pastry to make a lid. Wet the edges of the pastry lining the basin. Attach the lid of pastry. Steam the pudding for 1½ hours. Serve with custard.

FRUIT FOOL

Ingredients: 1 lb. stewed or bottled fruit, 2½ level tablespoons Household Milk, dry, 3 level tablespoons jam. *Quantity*: 4 helpings. *Method*: Strain the fruit and keep the juice for a sauce or jelly. Mash the fruit and mix with the milk and jam. Beat well. Serve in individual dishes topped with jam or custard.

PEACH JUNKET

Ingredients: 6 level tablespoons Household Milk, ¾ pint warm water, 4 heaped teaspoons peach jam, rennet 1½ times the usual quantity. *Quantity*: 4 helpings. *Method*: Put a heaped teaspoon of jam into 4 small dishes or cups. Reconstitute the milk with water and heat till warm to the touch add the rennet to the milk, stir and pour at once into the dishes. This junket can of course be made with fresh milk (¾ pint) using the usual quantity of rennet.

PRESERVES AND SUGAR COUPONS

You now have six coupons every four weeks to buy either preserves or sugar. They are the four sugar coupons and the two coupons marked P and R, both of which are in the sugar section of coupons. Each of these six coupons is worth either 1 lb. preserves or ½ lb. sugar. This means that you can buy as much as 6 lbs. preserves OR as much as 3 lbs. sugar. But as you will probably want both preserves and sugar, remember that you use one coupon for every 1 lb. of jam, and two coupons for every 1 lb. of sugar.

JAM BUNS

Ingredients: 1½ oz. margarine, 1 tablespoon jam, 1 dried egg, reconstituted, 3 heaped tablespoons self-raising flour. *Quantity*: 12 buns. *Method*: Cream margarine and jam together, add the reconstituted egg and flour. Bake in a hot oven from 10 to 15 minutes. This recipe can also be used to make 1 flat cake. In this case bake in a moderate oven for 15 to 20 minutes.

LISTEN TO THE KITCHEN FRONT ON TUESDAY, WEDNESDAY, THURSDAY & FRIDAY at 8.15 a.m.

Y.M.C.A. tea car personnel ready to serve the crews of gun and barrage balloon sites.

Fresh air food.

A mobile canteen presented to the Church Army by Sir Ernest and Lady Canning, 25th March 1941.

Where to get your new Ration Book

WHERE to go in BIRMINGHAM

WHEN—26th JUNE to 1st JULY, 1944

HOURS: MONDAYS to FRIDAYS; 9 a.m. to 6.30 p.m.
SATURDAYS - - - 9 a.m. to 4.0 p.m.

LOCAL DISTRIBUTION CENTRES CLOSE JULY 1st, 1944

WEEK 6—JUNE 26th to JULY 1st, 1944					
MON.	TUES.	WED.	THURS.	FRI.	SAT.
Ta-Th	Ti-TzU	Wa-We	Wh-Wi	Wo-Wz	VXYZ

1	CITY	Civic Centre
2	,,	Kent Street (Gala) Bath
3	,,	Northwood Street Baths
4	ASTON	Victoria Road Baths
5	ACOCKS GREEN	Westley Rd. Schools (Warwick Rd. Ent.)
6	BORDESLEY GREEN	Bordesley G. School, Marchmont Rd.
7	BALSALL HEATH	Moseley Road Baths
8	BIRCHFIELD	Birchfield Road School
9	ERDINGTON	Fire Station, Orphanage Road
10		Slade Road School
11	GREAT BARR	Beeches Road School
12	GOSTA GREEN	Woodcock Street Baths
13	HARBORNE	Harborne Baths
14	HANDSWORTH	Grove Lane Baths
15	HALL GREEN	Hall Green School, Stratford Road
16	KING'S HEATH	King's Heath Baths, Institute Road
17	KING'S NORTON	King's Norton School, The Green, Pershore Road
18	KINGSTANDING	Kingstanding Baths, Warren Farm Road
19	LADYWOOD	Monument Road Baths
20	NECHELLS	Nechells Baths, Nechells Park Road
21	NORTHFIELD	Northfield Baths, Bristol Rd. South
22	SALTLEY	Saltley Baths, George Arthur Road
23	SMALL HEATH	Green Lane Baths
24	SPARKHILL	Sparkhill Baths, Stratford Road
25	STECHFORD	Audley Road Schools
26	STIRCHLEY	Bournville Lane Baths
27	SELLY OAK	Tiverton Road Baths
28	WARD END	Sladefield Road School
29	WINSON GREEN	Dudley Road School
30	YARDLEY	Church Road School

Any person who attends a Distribution Centre may collect Ration Books for others outside the alphabetical range allotted for the day.

Factories, Firms and large Organisations may, as in previous years, participate in the "Block Scheme" by arranging in writing direct with the Food Executive Officer. All envelopes should be marked at top left-hand corner "Block Scheme." **D. LEWIS GRANT, Food Executive Officer.**

WEEK SIX. **SOLIHULL**
Food Office, 583, Warwick Road (Midland Red stop), where books for any initial may still be obtained.
OLTON
191, Warwick Road, Home Guard Office, near Station.
Monday, I J K.   Tuesday, L M N   Wednesday, O P Q.
Thursday, R S.   Friday, T U V   Saturday, W X Y Z.
Hours of Issue, 10 a.m. to 6 p.m. (Saturdays, 10 a.m. to 5 p.m.). Closed Daily from 1 p.m. to 2 p.m.
KNOWLE
Men's Institute, High Street. Commence July 3, 1944.
SUTTON COLDFIELD
Issue of Ration Books from the Town Hall and other special distribution points has now ceased.
Anyone who has not yet received their new book should apply without delay at the Food Office, Lloyd's Bank Chambers, High Street, Sutton Coldfield, 9 a.m. to 5.30 p.m., Monday to Friday, and 9 a.m. to 12.30 p.m. Saturdays.
RURAL DISTRICT OF BROMSGROVE
For details and particulars of distribution, see Posters in Cinemas, Shops, Post Offices, etc

---

WHAT TO DO *before you go to the Distribution Office*

1 Your Identity Card must be signed with your name on the inside in the space marked "Holder's Signature." It should also have your present permanent address on it. If it has not, or if you have lost your card, go at once to your local National Registration Office (same address as the Food Office) taking your present Ration Book with you. Remember, it's no use going to a Ration Book distribution office if your Identity Card is lost or incorrect.

2 Page 3 of your PRESENT RATION BOOK has been left blank so far. This must be filled in now. (The page is not to be cut out.) Then, on page 36 of your present Ration Book, make sure that the names and addresses of your retailers are written or stamped in the spaces provided.

Note: Take your Identity Card and present Ration Book with you when you go to get your new Book. If you are getting anyone else's Book, take his or her Identity Card and Ration Book properly filled in, too.

If you are an expectant mother and are due to go to the Food Office between May 22nd and July 23rd to get your Green Ration Book renewed, you can get your new Ration Books at the same time and so save yourself a second journey. Holders of temporary (yellow) Identity Cards who have to apply for extension during this period can also get their Ration Books at the same time.

The Birmingham Mail Fund clothing distribution, 29th November 1940.

The Lord Mayor, Alderman Wiggins-Davies, and the acting Lady Mayoress, his daughter Joan, supervise the distribution of gifts sent by the American Junior Red Cross to children of P.O.W's.

Public Health Department visit, 14th May 1941.

The cot maintained by the crew of "HMS Birmingham" at the Children's Hospital, 27th August 1941.

15

EVERY LITTLE HELPS

THEN UP I CAME WITH MY LITTLE LOT

. . . Never before have the Fighting Services of Great Britain, the Dominions and our Allies faced greater trials and responsibilities than to-day.

. . . Never before have we, the civilians on the Home Front, been called upon in so critical a time to give of our best in every way.

. . . In comparison with those risking their lives for us there are few things that we civilians can do at a time such as this. But those things *must* be done, and every penny, every shilling and every pound must be invested in War Savings if we are to achieve our goal of £14,000,000.

LIONEL G. H. ALLDRIDGE,
Lord Mayor

ROWANS OF NEW STREET give this space as a token of their deep gratitude to all ranks in our magnificent Armies.

£15,703,441 IN BIRMINGHAM'S "SALUTE" WEEK

FINAL FIGURES TO BE ANNOUNCED ON THURSDAY

CHANCELLOR'S TRIBUTE TO THE CITIZENS

26/6/44

The amount raised by Birmingham in "Salute the Soldier" Week was £15,703,441. This exceeded the target by £1,703,441. It was made clear by the Chancellor of the Exchequer, who announced the result on Saturday, that this is "not the final figure" and that other money "already contributed" has to be brought into calculation. The final figure will be announced by the Lord Mayor at the Civic Centre on Thursday afternoon.

BRAVO, BIRMINGHAM!

You're doing splendidly, but there's still a long way to go! If you have already invested, help us by seeing that all your friends and relations have invested too . . . and if you have not yet done your share, DO IT NOW!

BIRMINGHAM'S WINGS FOR VICTORY
JUNE 26 – JULY 3

Issued by Birmingham Savings Committee.

Miss Florence Faulkner, aged 62, purchases the millionth certificate issued by her firm's National Savings Group and here she presents it to one of the youngest employees, 15 yr-old Miss Doreen Turner. Miss Faulkner had, up to this point, been employed by the company for over 33 years. In the Boer War she made rifle clips, in the Great War she was engaged on shell production and finally, in the Second World War, she is involved in secret work for the war effort.

Joseph Lucas Ltd.

WINGS for VICTORY

invested for Employees Funds
£225,000

invested by company
£100,000

Employees Target for Week
£40,000

TOTAL LUCAS EFFORT
£365,000

R.A.F. VICTORY BELL APPEAL

Souvenir bells made from German aircraft shot down over Britain are now being sold in aid of the R.A.F. Benevolent Fund.

OUR WAR BABY

"We're saying 'thank you pal' by putting all we can into War Savings"

LET'S SAVE AS HARD AS THEY FIGHT

Issued by the National Savings Committee

INVEST YOUR SAVINGS

£ 10,000,000

WANTED FOR —

BIRMINGHAM'S WARSHIP WEEK

OCT. 18TH – 26TH

for

H.M.S. KING GEORGE V.

WHICH WILL BE ADOPTED BY BIRMINGHAM.

INVEST everything you can in SAVINGS BONDS; NATIONAL WAR BONDS; DEFENCE BONDS; SAVINGS CERTIFICATES.

DEPOSIT more in P.O. SAVINGS BANK; BIRMINGHAM MUNICIPAL BANK.

ISSUED BY THE BIRMINGHAM SAVINGS COMMITTEE.

Give your "mite" for Warship "might"

EVERYTHING WELCOME!

"We're doing splendidly—we've passed our fuel target already!"

Look around all the corners and help the rubber salvage campaign!

Salvage collection at 30 Rotton Park Road, the home of the Lady Mayoress, Mrs Elvira Martineau, 1941.

A.R.P. Wardens of D. Division (South) outside the entrance to Aston Hall.

A.R.P. Wardens at Soho Road, Handsworth, 1942.

19

Gas Board employees, Margaret Street.

The March Past of the Girl Guides at their annual church parade at Kings Norton Parish Church, taken by Dame Elizabeth Cadbury, 3rd June 1940.

Younger members of the Birmingham City Police Force released to join the Forces in July, 1942.

Women's Auxillary Police Corps.

St John's Ambulance Parade, 27th August 1944, along Colmore Row.

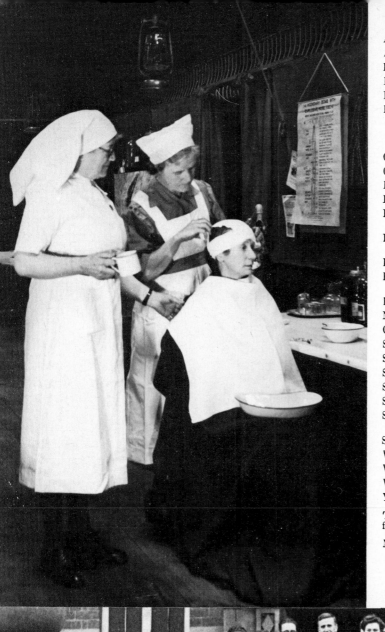

FIRST AID POSTS.

ASTON.	Aston Baths, Victoria Road.
ACOCK'S GREEN.	Westley Road School.
BORDESLEY GREEN.	Bordesley Green School, Marchmont Road.
BALSALL HEATH.	Moseley Road Baths.
BIRCHFIELD.	Birchfield Road School.
ERDINGTON.	Erdington Baths, Mason Road.
	Bromford Child Welfare Centre, Tyburn Road.
	Slade Road School.
GREAT BARR.	Beeches Road School.
GOSTA GREEN.	Woodcock Street Baths.
HARBORNE	Harborne Baths, Lordswood Road.
HANDSWORTH.	Handsworth Baths, Grove Lane.
HALL GREEN.	Hall Green School, Stratford Road, near Highfield Road.
HIGHTER'S HEATH.	Highter's Heath School, Highter's Heath Lane.
KING'S HEATH.	King's Heath Baths, Institute Road.
KING'S NORTON.	King's Norton School, The Green, Pershore Road South.
KINGSTANDING.	Kingstanding Baths, Warren Farm Road.
NORTHFIELD.	Northfield Baths, Bristol Road South.
QUINTON.	Woodhouse Road School.
SALTLEY.	Saltley Baths, George Arthur Road.
SMALL HEATH.	Small Heath Baths, Green Lane.
SPARKHILL.	Sparkhill Baths, Stratford Road.
SHELDON.	Stanville Road School.
STECHFORD.	Audley Road School.
STIRCHLEY.	Stirchley Child Welfare Centre, Charlotte Road.
SELLY OAK.	Tiverton Road Baths.
WARD END.	Sladefield Road School.
WEOLEY CASTLE.	Paganel Road School.
WINSON GREEN.	Dudley Road School.
YARDLEY.	Church Road School.

The foregoing Bathing Establishments are still available for normal facilities.

MASONIC BUILDING,
BROAD STREET,
BIRMINGHAM, 1.

D. LEWIS GRANT,
FOOD EXECUTIVE OFFICER.
4th NOVEMBER, 1941.

First aid post, Handsworth Baths.

SISTER TO ASSIST 'ER

A National Domestic Help service on the lines of the District Nursing service to bring temporary help to all who need it, was foreshadowed by Mr. Bevin, Minister of Labour, in the House of Commons yesterday.

OLD BILL AND YOUNG BILL

Men disabled in this war get lower pensions than are still being paid to those whose injuries were sustained in a war which ended nearly 25 years ago.

Green Lane first aid post at Small Heath Baths. Albert Judd (2nd right back row), who provided this photograph, was awarded the National Commendation Medal for rescuing 15 horses from Whitmore Road coal stables on the night of 20th November 1940.

THE STONEHOUSE GANG

HARRY WEBB

"It seemed to me that, with the absence of Dads because of the war, there was a particular need to fill this void. So we developed the Stonehouse Gang, centred on an estate where there was no provision for boys.

We later included girls as well and the Gang is still going strong today."

In 1941 the lads build their H.Q. on the corner of Swinford Road and Stonehouse Hill, Selly Oak, from an old fowl house, a tennis pavilion and a custard powder workship.

The opening of the completed premises. The hut was situated on the opposite corner to a barrage balloon site. HARRY WEBB is seen 6th from right.

Reg Jones the first lad to join up, returns on leave from the Navy to wish Bill Flint good luck in the RAF.

ANIMALS AT WAR

The Second World War is usually seen as a highly mechanised affair and it might come as a surprise to some that more horses were used by the participants than in the Great War. On the Russian Front alone, the Red Army had 1,200,000 horses employed in various tasks, including 30 cavalry divisions, and much of the German artillery was horse-or ox-drawn. Mules too were used in large numbers - 20,000 in the Hellenic campaign, 13,000 by the Allies in Italy, and 3,000 served with Wingate's Chindits in Burma. RAF Coastal and Bomber Commands used homing pigeons for emergency purposes. If a plane was in difficulty a pigeon was released carrying details to aid the rescuers. In fact, homing pigeons were protected under the Defence of the Realm Act, and to shoot one could result in the miscreant being jailed for 6 months or fined £100. Falcons were used to clear airfields of smaller birds. However, the Royal Navy failed in its attempt to train seagulls to obscure U-boat periscopes with their droppings.

Animals and The Home Front

In the first days following the declaration of war, the animal welfare organisations were inundated with requests from cat and dog owners to have their pets put down. Between the 3rd-7th September there were 400,000 requests from pet owners in London alone! Pet owners' problems were compounded when rationing was introduced. Working horses, goats, cattle and chickens were allocated protein rations, and warehouse cats and mousers eventually received a dried milk ration. Hay was never rationed and many pet owners queued for hours at a time to buy horse meat for their dogs and cats. Between 1939-1945, the RSPCA, PDSA, Canine Defence League and National ARP for Animals Committee rescued a combined total of 256,000 animals and birds from bombing raids. During the worst of the bombing people were issued with shelter cards to pin on their gateposts to show they would make room for owners and their dogs caught out walking during an air-alert. Pet owners were issued with yet another card to put outside their house on which they recorded how many people and how many animals were resident, and whereabouts they usually slept, so that rescue squads had some idea where to start looking in the event of the house being hit.

Pony in a gas mask.

A volunteer helper at the Horse's Rest, Barnes Hill, Weoley Castle.

"Sputum" the horse helps with the hay-making at the City Sanatorium, Small Heath.

Rommel's horse ridden by Montgomery's groom after its capture. The photograph was taken by a member of the band of the Royal Warks. Regt.

Dogs' anti-gas chamber.

The PDSA to the rescue

Dogs' air raid shelter.

ALFA AND ADA CROWSON:
"As soon as the sirens went, on the night of 19th November 1940, we put our budgie Jackie in her cage and left her in the pantry while we went down to the Anderson shelter. The house in Burbury Street, Lozells, was almost completely destroyed that night, but somehow Jackie survived and gave us a very big welcome when we unearthed her."

Bobby II antelope mascot of the 2nd bn Royal Warks. Regt.

On 3rd March 1941 the Lord Mayor, Alderman Wilfrid Martineau, presented RSPCA awards to several people who had "rescued animals from positions of peril arising out of enemy action", including a bronze medal and certificate to Frank Bennett, who had stood for over 5 hours in the River Rea in order to calm 2 frightened horses blown from their stables by a bomb blast.

One of the most stirring examples of heroism was that of Marion Almond and Maurice Jones who, whilst on duty at the RSPCA centre in Bristol Road, extinguished over 60 incendiaries, gave first aid to firemen and other people, and then, after loading 17 cats, 8 dogs and a canary into an ambulance, drove them 4 miles, under terrible conditions, to safety. They were both awarded the Margaret Wheatley Cross and Certificate.

Silver medals and certificates went to night watchman Victor Leverington who had liberated dozens of kittens, fowls, ducks and rabbits when the Market Hall was hit, and to P.C Richard Tunstall, whose persistence resulted in the rescue of a dog trapped in sewers.

(Left to right) Frank Bennett, Maurice Jones, Marion Almond, Victor Leverington and P.C. Richard Tunstall with the Lord Mayor.

WAR PRODUCTION

TRADING WITH THE ENEMY

NOTICE TO TRADERS AND OTHERS.

1. Traders, shipowners and others are warned that as from the outbreak of war it is unlawful to transact business or to have other dealings with enemies without official permission (which will not be granted save in exceptional circumstances). Offenders will be liable to heavy penalties.

2. For the purpose of this notice the term " enemy " may be, assumed to cover:—

> (*a*) Governmental agencies in enemy territory;
>
> (*b*) any person or business resident or established in enemy territory;
>
> (*c*) any branch (in any country) controlled from a principal place of business in enemy territory; and
>
> (*d*) any company or other body of persons which is constituted or incorporated under enemy law.

It does **not,** however, include any person by reason only that he is a national of an enemy country. " **Enemy territory " includes any territory in the occupation of the enemy's armed forces.**

3. In particular, traders and other persons are warned:—

> (i) Not to pay, lend or send money, negotiable instruments or securities to or for the benefit of an enemy or to a place in enemy territory or enter into, continue or complete any transaction which will enable an enemy to obtain money or credit or any transaction which will release an enemy from an obligation to pay money;
>
> (ii) Not to discharge any debt due to an enemy (including debts on bills of exchange) which the enemy has assigned to a neutral assignee;
>
> (iii) Not to accept any payment from an enemy of a sum of money due in respect of a transaction unless all obligations on the part of the person receiving payment had been completed before the outbreak of war;
>
> (iv) Not to supply any goods to an enemy or for the benefit of an enemy; not to obtain any goods from an enemy; and not to trade in, or carry, any goods consigned to or from an enemy or destined for or coming from enemy territory.

R.A.F. 99128

MINISTRY OF SUPPLY
CONTRACT NO. 294/23/P/3611/CON.
RADAR VEHICLE TYPE 461
Built by
METROPOLITAN-CAMMELL CARRIAGE & WAGON C
1944
HO.10577.   NEG. N

NEWMAN TONKS

29

THIS
CERTIFICATE OF HONOUR
IS AWARDED TO

Wм. Newman & Sons Lᴛᴰ

SAVINGS GROUP
IN RECOGNITION OF SPECIAL ACHIEVEMENT
DURING THE

WINGS FOR VICTORY
NATIONAL SAVINGS CAMPAIGN 1943

I EXTEND MY THANKS TO ALL CONCERNED
IN THIS IMPORTANT NATIONAL SERVICE.

Archibald Sinclair
SECRETARY OF STATE FOR AIR

Birmingham
Weekly Post
FRIDAY, AUGUST 29, 1941

WOMEN OF BIRMINGHAM

VICTORY
IS IN YOUR HANDS

Britain, the Forces, the whole world are looking to Birmingham to set the lead in the great arms drive that will bring victory. The machines are ready . . some of them standing idle waiting for *you* to work them. The factories of Birmingham want every Birmingham woman who is not on really vital War Work.

Ask yourself if *you* are doing all you can. If not, nothing must stand in your way—even though the work may be hard or dirty, and means leaving a "nicer" position or seeing less of your home. Every one of us can do something—every one of us *must*—and now's the time !

Aircraft gun turrets, final assembly.

Mobile infromation bureau set up to try and persuade women to undertake some form of war work.

Preparing for heat treatment brass strip used for cartridge cases.

Sheet metal at Kynochs.

Bofors shell cases made at the Kynoch Works of ICI Metals Division, now part of IMI.

Above: the King visits Kynochs, 1939.

Below: The Duke of Kent meets Austin workers.

33

A completed Stirling bomber, Austin.

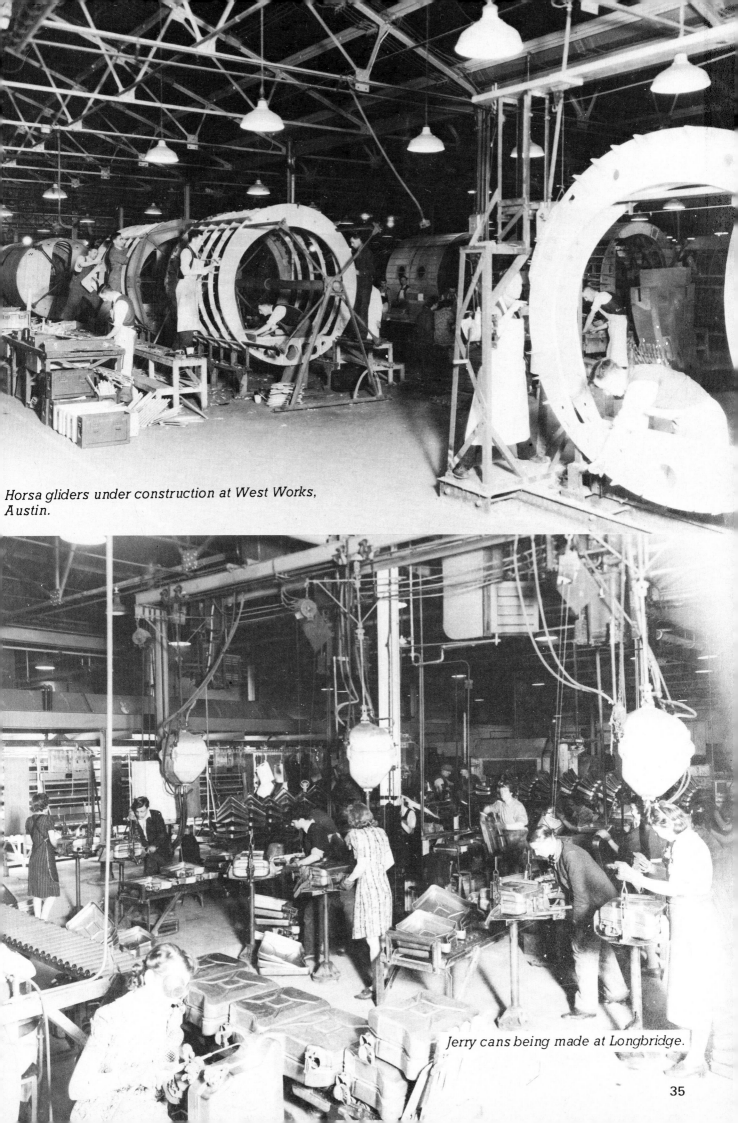

Horsa gliders under construction at West Works,
Austin.

Jerry cans being made at Longbridge.

Lucas's Shaftmoor Lane.

Lucas's Great King Street.

During their summer vacation a number of boys, from various schools, assisted the war effort by working in factories.

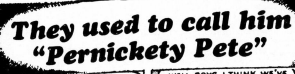

They used to call him "Pernickety Pete"

MORAL: A lighted match or cigarette-end can do as much harm as an incendiary bomb. Every other minute a fire breaks out somewhere in Britain — and most of these fires are started by people who never started a fire before. Everyone should make certain their matches and cigarette-ends are really out when they throw them away.

You çan't be too careful!

JOHN TAYLOR:
"I was an apprentice at Chance Bros. and an ex-World War I Major instructed me to make several knobkerries out of steam pipe with a 6-inch solid spike screwed into the end, to use as a means of repelling any enemy invaders."

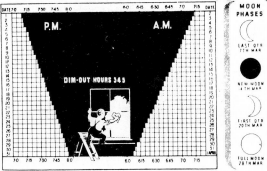

Above: Shell production

Below: Working on Bren Gun magazines.

The girls get things moving!

Mrs. Eleanor Roosevelt, wife of the American President, watches test pilots, 7th November, 1942. The Regional Commissioner, Lord Dudley, is on the right.

These stills are from a film, for one of the ministries, called 'Taking the Work to the Worker'. They show 'outworkers' involved in the simple assembly of components used in armaments.

Make the most of small plots

Those who have not the time, strength or available land to cultivate the standard 10-rod plot, should get the latest free Ministry of Agriculture Leaflet. It is a Cropping Plan designed for a space 45 x 30 ft. (5 rods) —roughly the size of the average garden. It is based on the essential wartime principle of making sure of winter greens (though of course it provides for some vegetables all the year round), and contains a coloured plan and a table of planting.

REMINDERS

If you have not sown Brussels Sprouts and Leeks in the seed-bed, order some plants now so that you will be sure of having some when planting-out time comes. Sow Spinach Beet and Seakale Beet in groups 1 in. deep and 8 in. apart. Single later. Sow the first row of maincrop Peas— 3 in.-4 in. apart, 2 in. deep.

PART 1 IN THE POTATO PLAN

Parsley Potato Cakes

Potatoes for Breakfast
three days a week

Potatoes taste grand for breakfast. Try them! Here's a good suggestion: Parsley Potato Cakes. Are you watching out for other recipes in this series?

PARSLEY POTATO CAKES

Boil an extra pound of potatoes the day before you want to make the cakes. Mash these while hot, with a little milk, and seasoning of salt and pepper to taste.

Next day, add a tablespoon of chopped parsley and shape the mixture into little cakes. Cover with browned breadcrumbs, and pan-fry in a little hot fat, or bake in the oven. The mixture should not be made wet.

The 4 other parts of the Plan:

2 Make your main dish a potato dish one day a week.

3 Refuse second helpings of other food. Have more potatoes instead.

4 Serve potatoes in other ways than " plain boiled."

5 Use potatoes in place of flour (part potatoes, part flour).

Bread costs ships . . .
Eat home-grown potatoes instead

ISSUED BY THE MINISTRY OF FOOD, LONDON, W.1
P.24   "B Post"   16/2/43

NATURE CONTRIBUTES TO THE WAR EFFORT!

DIG FOR VICTORY

CASTLE BROMWICH AEROPLANE FACTORY

As rearmament got into its stride, one of the priorities was the modernisation of the RAF which, in 1937, had only a handful of squadrons equipped with modern combat aircraft.

In 1938 a large shadow factory was built at Castle Bromwich designed to greatly increase fighter output by the second half of 1940 and to be able to meet demand in the the event of war. At the outset it was concerned with the manufacture of Fairey Battles. Originally placed under Nuffield management, the plant was put under the control of Vickers, the parent company of the Spitfire, in May, 1940. Up to June, 1940, Spitfires had been assembled solely at Vickers Supermarine, Southampton. When Castle Bromwich came on line, the west midlands plant worked up to an output of 320 aircraft a month - a record for any type of aircraft in the U.K.

In 1943 Lancaster bombers were also produced, but this reduced the scale of efficiency of manufacture. Also produced at Castle Bromwich was the Seafire, a naval variant of the Spitfire.

THE POPULAR PLANE

The Lord Mayor of Birmingham has opened a fund for the purchase of Spitfires.

Churchill meets Chief Test Pilot Captain Alec Henshaw.

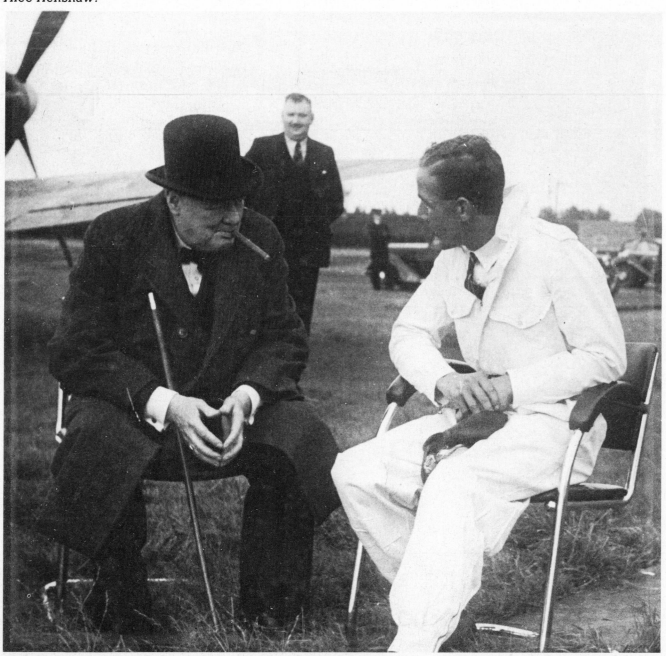

"E" Block Surpervisors including, third from left, back row, Alton's father.

A Spitfire standing on the apron.

FRED DORRELL:
"Supermarine Works at Southampton, the original manufacturers of the Spitfire, were
badly hit and the Air Ministry gave instructions that certain experienced aircraft fitters
should be transferred from Austin Aero to Castle Bromwich to help speed up the production
of the Spitfires. I moved to 'E' block in 1940."

"E" Block with everything jigged up for fast production This is one of those
photographs, referred to on Page 3, that should not have been taken.

44

ENTERTAINING THE WORKERS

Lucas employees lead a lunchtime sing-song.

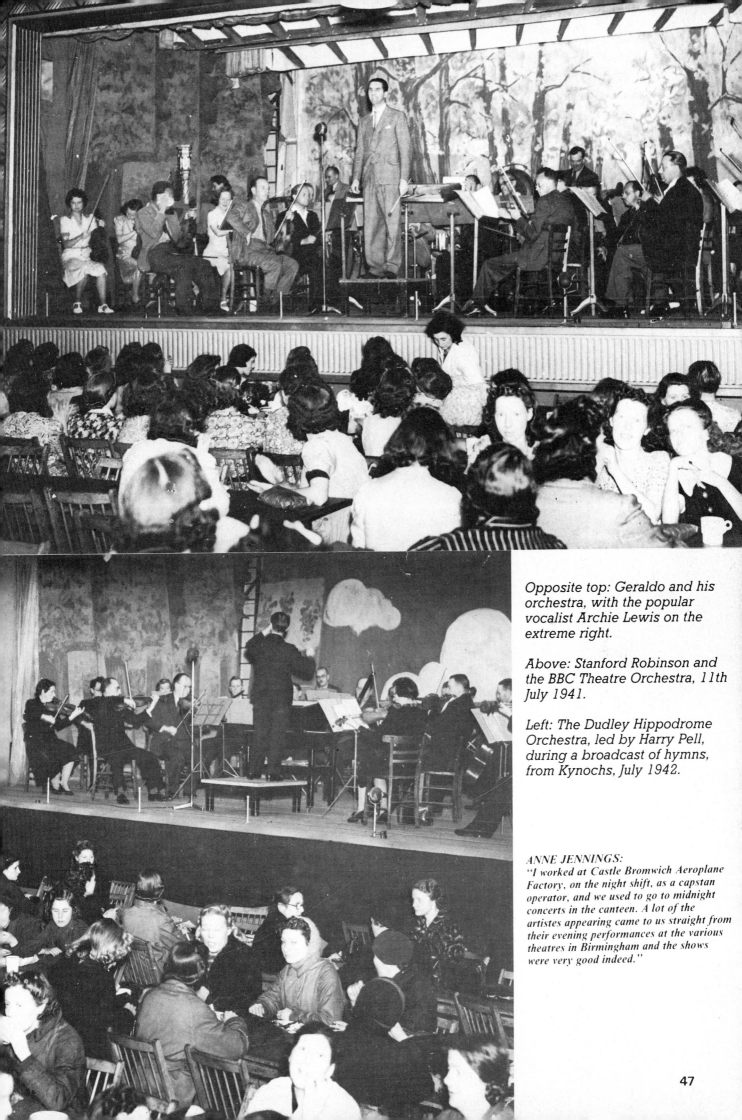

Opposite top: Geraldo and his orchestra, with the popular vocalist Archie Lewis on the extreme right.

Above: Stanford Robinson and the BBC Theatre Orchestra, 11th July 1941.

Left: The Dudley Hippodrome Orchestra, led by Harry Pell, during a broadcast of hymns, from Kynochs, July 1942.

ANNE JENNINGS:
"I worked at Castle Bromwich Aeroplane Factory, on the night shift, as a capstan operator, and we used to go to midnight concerts in the canteen. A lot of the artistes appearing came to us straight from their evening performances at the various theatres in Birmingham and the shows were very good indeed."

HIS MASTER'S VOICE

THE MAN WHO FOR US IS THE GREATEST IN THE WORLD — OUR FUHRER.

Top Left: The Birmingham Hippodrome Orchestra.

Left: The RAF Band.

Below: W. Canning's Concert Party, June, 1940

48

Above: Gracie Fields plays to a packed a house at Kynochs, 5th August 1941.

Below: Kynoch Follies.

FIRE!

By 1937 Birmingham possessed one of the most efficient and best equipped fire brigades in the country, capable of dealing with any peace-time emergency. However, the deepening crisis in Central Europe and the possibility of war breaking out forced the authorities to make plans. It was soon realised that a serious air raid would overwhelm the Brigade's resources and that help would have to be sought from ordinary civilians, or, even better, civilians trained as fire-fighters.

On 15th August 1937, the Auxillary Fire Service was formed in the city and by the end of the year some 2,000 men had been enlisted. As the international situation deteriorated during 1939, uniforms were issued, trailer pumps delivered, and the recruiting drive stepped up. On the 9th Augsut, a text blackout was held with the A.F.S. being called out to deal with 9 air raid 'fires'.

The first air raid alert sounded on the evening of the 3rd September and resulted in chaos in the engine-house at Headquarters. Orders in the event of air raids were that the crew of the first pump should be equipped in full anti-gas rig; the crew of the second pump to wear gas trousers and unform jacket; and the other crews to be in uniform plus gas masks and steal helmets. It was dark in the engine-house with the men groping around for their uniforms and equipment. When the Divisional Officer turned on the lights, he was met by the sight of numerous firemen in various stages of dress, and, standing in the middle of what must have looked like the Mad Hatter's tea party, was one fireman dressed only in his birthday suit. When asked what he was doing, our stark naked fire-fighter stood to attention and said "I am sorry, sir, but I am waiting for you to make up your mid whether we are dressing for dinner or for firefighting."

By the end of 1939, A.F.S. strength stood at 11,849 men, 178 stations and 535 trailer pumps pulled by an assortment of vehicles ranging from old taxis to Austin 8's and even Rolls-Royces.

On 1st January 1940, Divisional Officer Coleman was appointed officer in charge of the A.F.S. and he set about bringing his auxilliaries up to standard with the regular brigade, and following Dunkirk a Home Guard A.F.S. battalion was formed.

The night of the 24/25th October witnessed a heavy raid on the city. Soon there were 189 major fires raging and although 371 appliances were at work, reinforcements had to be called in with 84 pumps and crews coming from the East Midlands and Reading. The crews were still making up when the sirens went again on the night of the 25th. The following night the sirens went shortly after 7 p.m. Holloway Head was hit and there were serious fires in Constitution Hill. By midnight 276 fires were raging in the city and 548 pumps were at work. 111 pumps and crews were drafted into the city to help out. A.F.S. casualites for the 2 nights were 5 killed and 111 injured.

Reinforcement was not all one-way. Officers and men were often sent to the aid of other towns. On the morning of the 15th November, 20 pumps were sent to the aid of Coventry, and at various times crews were sent to the aid of Manchester, Liverpool, Plymouth and Portsmouth.

On the night of 19/20th November, the Luftwaffe once again turned its attention to Birmingham causing 425 fires, many of which took hours to bring under control. The night of 22/23rd November saw the Coventration of Birmingham. The raid started shortly before 7 p.m., the all-clear not sounding until shortly before 6 a.m. With 3 water mains in the Bristol Road fractured by H.E. bombs, the city was soon without water except for what could be obtained from some undamaged canals and from bomb craters.

The night of 9/10th April 1941 saw another heavy raid on the city. The whole of the Midland Arcade was a mass of flames and the fire-fighters could not prevent flames jumping the width of New Street and setting buildings in Worcester Street alight. At one point a sea of blazing tar began to push its way downhill towards New Street station, and senior fire officers called in the Royal Engineers to blast a firebreak. However, before the fuses could be lit, a large building collapsed, cutting off the fires.

National Fire Services

On 13th May 1941, Home Secretary Herbert Morrison announced his nationalisation plan to Parliament and within a week the Fire Service (Emergency Provisions) Bill, 1941, became law. On 18th August the independent brigades ceased to exist and the National Fire Service came into being. The A.F.S. was incorporated into the new organisation. Birmingham was now classed as part of No. 2 Fire Force along with Coventry, Rugby, Redditch and certain Black Country towns.

On the night of the 27/28th July 1942, the N.F.S. had its baptism of fire. With 263 fires raging in the west and southern parts of the city, 468 pumps were at work.

With the tide of war turning, 899 officers and men of No. 24 Fire Force were sent south to reinforce the invasion posts in case of retaliatory raids. After D-Day the strength of the Fire Force was gradually reduced and by V.E. Day was nearly down to its peace-time establishment.

By the end of the war, Birmingham A.F.S. had lost 20 men killed and many badly wounded. Station Officer Mosedale had been awarded the George Cross after rescuing 6 trapped firemen from their station after it had taken a direct hit. Other awards included 1 OBE, 1MBE, 4 George Medals and 3 BEM's.

Putting out a petrol fire. Midland Red A.R.P. fire fighting demonstration, 1939.

Cornwall Street.

Moseley Street.

Winners of 'B' Divison Pump Drill shield at the Spot Garage, Bristol Road South, Northfield, 1940.

53

ADVICE TO CONSUMERS

In the event of an Air Raid :—

(1) Draw sufficient water in clean receptacles for immediate drinking requirements. If the house is fitted with a bath this might be filled to say, one-third of its capacity, to act as a reserve supply for washing and sanitary purposes.

(2) When a reserve supply has been drawn, turn off the water at the inside stopcock, if any, so as to prevent flooding, etc., if the inside pipes and fittings should be damaged.

(Find out beforehand where this stopcock is.)

(3) If water supply fails, put out the fire serving the hot water system as soon as possible.

(4) Economise in use of water generally, as large quantities may be required for fire fighting, essential supplies, and decontamination purposes.

A. E. FORDHAM
Secretary

Water Department Offices
Council House,
Edmund Street,
Birmingham.
September, 1939.

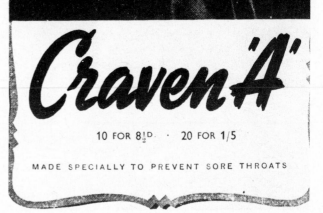

Left: A rehearsal for tackling fire bombs.

AFS, December, 1939.

Voluntary auxilliary firewomen at Lucas.

Birmingham Mail, 9th November 1942:
"The first N.F.S. wedding took place on Saturday. We have always contended that the N.F.S. was a dangerous job."

MONDAY, JANUARY 5, 1942

"STATIC WATER"

The emergency fire-fighting reservoir, holding about 650,000 gallons, which has been completed in Duddeston Row, Birmingham. It is a good example of the huge tanks which have been built all over Birmingham and other cities for use in future air raids. These civil defence reservoirs in Birmingham are usually six or eight feet deep, but vary a great deal in area and hold anything between 150,000 and nearly a million gallons.

SIR STEPHEN BURMAN

Mr Stephen Burman (now Sir Stephen) joined the Selly Oak and Kings Norton Division of the Auxillary Fire Service in 1937 as an ordinary Auxillary Fireman and his first experience of fighting fires caused by enemy action was in that area.

He was moved to Central Headquarters, eventually becoming Head of the A.F.S., with responsibility for the mobilisation of the fire fighting forces throughout the region (5 counties in all).

With the integration of the regular and auxillary services Mr Burman was an Assistant Fire Force Commander, being second in command for the region. It was for his work in the Fire Service that he was awarded the M.B.E.

The Fire Force Headquarters kept closely in touch with th R.A.F. and the Army, and it is recalled how decoy on fires were created in the open country so that enemy bombers would mistake them for fires started in a town by an earlier flight of their own "marker" planes. This did meet with success.

There was a very worrying time when bombs dropped in Bristol Road fractured some of the 42-inch water mains from the Elan Valley and the city was virtually without water until repairs could be effected. It was extremely lucky that the enemy failed to return for some days, by which time the service had been restored and the fire fighters could operate again.

When Mr Burman's Division was dealing with a fire at Holloway Head they saw in the firelight a parachute bomb moving towards them. It was carried by wind and dropped elsewhere. The following morning Mr Burman had to submit a routine report to H.Q. and the only casualties listed concerned 2 broken noses and a broken arm suffered by firemen throwing themselves into the gutter when the bomb was seen.

One night when there was a series of fires in Corporation Street, C & A staff had come to their stores and a procession of them were seen carrying naked ladies out of the building to save them from melting. The "ladies" were, of course, display dummies!

Mr Burman's sister was a BBC announcer in London and when the first V1 rockets ("buzz bombs") came over she went onto the roof of Broadcasting House and recorded them. She brought the recording to Mr Burman, who played it to his staff at the Central Fire Station. Unfortunately the tannoy system was loud enough for the recording to be heard outside and people were alarmed, thinking that "buzz bombs" were over Birmingham.

A.F.S. centre in Cambridge Street, 19th February 1941.

HOME GUARD

On 14th May 1940, Anthony Eden, the Secretary of State for War, broadcast an appeal for men aged 17-65 to form a new home defence force to be known as the Local Defence Volunteers. There was no medical, but volunteers were to be 'vetted' to prevent Fifth Columnists from enlisting. Originally the L.D.V. was to have had no officers or N.C.O.'s in the usual sense, and this raised doubts as to whether or not the force qualified as irregulars under the terms of the Geneva Convention. The Germans reacted by calling the L.D.V. "murder bands" and said that when they invaded Britain L.D.V. members would be shot out of hand.

In July, 1940 the L.D.V. was officially christened the Home Guard. Not only were there units to protect districts, but many firms established companies to protect their premises. These factory units were independent private armies and were not integrated into the Home Guard until 1942. At its height, Birmingham's Home Guard stood at 53,000 men, the wooden rifles, walking sticks and clubs eventually giving way to rifles, machine guns, grenades and anti-tank weapons.

A Typical Home Guard Battlion

44th bn. Royal Warks. Regt. was formed in the Hockley area by 4 firms, each providing a company. These were W. Canning and Co. Ltd., Joseph Lucas Ltd., Bulpitt and Sons Ltd. and the Birmingham Mint, which was joined by a small firm, Thomas Fattorini Ltd.

Harry Reynolds, who has spent his working life at Canning's, had only recently started in the Buying Department when a meeting was first held amongst employees to organise themselves into a body of Local Defence Volunteers. The Head Buyer was going to be the Quartermaster Sergeant and he instructed Harry to get 144 broomsticks and take them to a factory of theirs in Constitution Hill, where the recruits, using the broomsticks, were drilled by men with experience in the regular army in the First World War.

Gradually uniforms and helmets became available. The first rifles were a dozen Lee Enfields from the First World War, and they arrived caked in black grease, which Harry spent a happy weekend removing.

One weapon the men learned to use later was the Northolt Projector. This was like a drainpipe that the operator placed on his shoulder and into which he inserted a small bottle primed with petrol. This was for firing at vehicles, such as tanks, at close range. A similar but more powerful device was the Blacka Bombard. It had a longer range and projected a fin-tailed high explosive bomb well over a foot long.

Each man attended one night in every 6 for instruction in such subjects as map reading, aircraft recognition and unarmed combat or for the demonstration of a new weapon. Of course a guard protecting the firm's premises would be maintained without interruption. In the event of an air raid, all members would immediately report for duty.

Manoeuvres took place at week-ends. A typical exercise was when some of the men positioned in the orchard of the "George-in-the-Tree" at Berkswell attempted to take Berkswell Hall. A great deal of blank ammunition was used.

Each company was divided into 2 units, one mobile and one static. In the event of an emergency, such as the landing of enemy paratroops in a certain area, the mobile unit would be sent to engage them, while the static unit kept guard at its own location.

Members of the Canning Home Guard

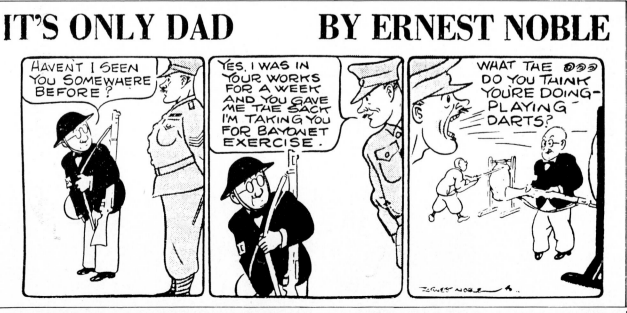

SHAPE

HP Sauce Home Guard Unit, 1941.

British Timken Home Guard Unit, 10th March 1943.

Mounted Home Guard caught off-guard!

Women's Mounted Home Guard.

JOHN HENRY LEWIS

Councillor John Lewis, now Alderman Lewis, known in many circles as "John Henry", played a major role in the Home Guard. Prevented from joining the regular forces by his work in the essential field of fuel distribution, he formed a group of the Home Guard consisting of corporation personnel, comprising staff of the Council House and of the various civic departments such as gas, electricity and water.

John Lewis was second in command of "A" Group, with the rank of Lt. Colonel, and was appointed Home Guard Liaison Officer for the Birmingham zone. It fell to him to organise parades for distinguished visitors, including Winston Churchill and General de Gaulle.

King Haakon of Norway was another, and a Norwegian adjutant in the Home Guard, hearing of the impending visit, expressed a keen desire to meet him. John Lewis arranged for the adjutant to lurk in a corner of the promenade at the bottom of the Council House steps, and after the king had inspected the guard of honour and was being escorted by the Home Guard Commander, Colonel Clive Piggott, into the Council House, the adjutant stepped smartly foward and was introduced to his king and a chat ensued that was enjoyed by both.

Mr Lewis recalls a zone shooting day at Frankley Reservoir. The chaplain, the Reverend Harry McGowan, Archdeacon of Aston, arrived on the scene and Colonel Piggott invited him to try his hand. The Archdeacon scored 5 bull's eyes in succession! It transpired that he was an experienced marksman, having shot regularly at Bisley.

A more serious memory for John Lewis was when he was on duty in the centre of the city and reports came in from the outskirts that German parachutists were landing. These proved to be land mines dropping by parachute.

His wife Joan, daughter of Alderman Wiggins-Davies, was enrolled in the Mounted Home Guard. This came about because parkland areas around the city, which were potential landing grounds for enemy paratroops, could be patrolled on horseback. Young women horse owners lent their horses to the Home Guard and patrolled Sutton Park themselves during daytime, the men doing the dawn and dusk patrols. There were 10 women and 25 men.

Home Guards on duty near a crater in a roadway after a bomb had blown out some shop fronts during last night's Midland raid.

Above: The corner of Green lane and Coventry Road, Small Heath, 17th October 1940.

Left: John Lewis, Liaison Officer of the Birmingham Zone Home Guard, greets General Charles de Gaulle, leader of the Free French, while Colonel J.C. Piggott, Zone Commander, looks on approvingly, 7th February 1942.

In the years when our Country

was in mortal danger

FREDERICK JAMES DORRELL

who served 20th January 1942 – 31st December 1944

gave generously of his time and

powers to make himself ready

for her defence by force of arms

and with his life if need be.

George R.I.

THE HOME GUARD

WAITING TO JOIN UP

Mail 5. 9. 39

Recruits learning Bren gun drill with the aid of a specially painted landscape, 31st October 1939.

Pioneer Corps recruiting campaign. 1940.

"All our aircraft returned safely . . ."
THESE WOMEN HELPED TO MAKE IT TRUE

Women of the WAAF help to make the weather reports on which the RAF boys rely

RON CATTON (Warks. Yeomanry):
"As we marched along Bradford Street to [the]
station the band was playing 'Warwickshi[re]
and Lassies', the girls were waving from [the]
windows and I had a great feeling of light[ness,]
excitement. It wasn't until much later th[at the]
enormity of it all really hit us."

Every job at an R.A.F. station is part of a pattern that can clearly be seen.

Every person working on the station realizes that he, or she, is part of the force that is being used on the side of Freedom. It is grand to know that.

And now, as the Offensive extends and every man who can fight is needed in the fighting lines, thousands more women are needed in the Services. If your present job is not genuinely helping the war effort, you can come into the WAAF or the ATS and *know* that there you will be putting your full weight behind the Offensive. Every woman who can be spared from civilian life is needed. Over 100 trades are open. Age limits are 17½ to 43; up to 50 for some trades.

If there are difficulties in your way, or if there are questions you must have answered before you can make up your mind, go to a Recruiting Centre* or Employment Exchange for advice, and information about types of work, pay, leave, etc. Or, if you send in the coupon (1d. stamp), information will be sent you. Do not delay !

ATS and WAAF Recruiting Centre :

Victoria Hall, Witton Road, Aston

* Single girls born between January 1st, 1918, and June 30th, 1922, come under the National Service Act and must go to their Employment Exchange, not to a Recruiting Centre.

THOUSANDS MORE LIKE THEM
are needed urgently in
the ATS and WAAF

7 Oxford Street, London, W.1.

Below: 70th bn Royal Warks Regt. a[t ...]
Barracks, Exeter, March 1943, led b[y ...]
Bates-Oldham. Primarily a young so[ldier]
battalion, the unit was eventually di[sbanded]
and many of the men took part in
Montgomery's Second Front.

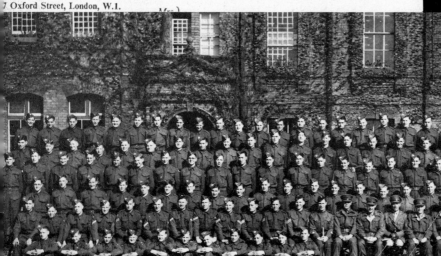

How the "Call-up" affects the Women of Britain

An official explanation of Registration and Compulsory Call-up

Single Women

Born in 1920 and 1921

The call-up will take place by stages. When you are called up will depend partly on your age, partly on the work you are doing.

You have been asked to say whether you would prefer the Services, whole-time Civil Defence or war industry. As far as possible your preference will be met, but what particular job you are required to take will depend on the national need at the time.

If your preference is for the Services you must wait now until you are called up, when you will get an enrolment notice. From January 10th, 1942, onwards, women born in 1920 and 1921 cannot themselves volunteer for the Women's Auxiliary Services.

If you choose industry you will get a direction and will probably be directed into a Royal Ordnance filling factory, but you may be able to go into other munition work, training for engineering, or agriculture, or hospital work if you are specially suited for it. You can volunteer for war industry at once if you wish, but you can only get a job through the Employment Exchange and you will have the same jobs to choose from as if you were being called up. ·

You will have to be prepared to leave home and go where you are sent, unless this would mean exceptional hardship.

If you have specialised skill or training you will be directed to work where it can best be used in the national interest.

If you are already in certain reserved work you will not be called up and in most cases you cannot leave without permission from the Ministry of Labour. The Exchange can tell you what this work is. If you do leave and are still available for work you will then have to state your preference as above.

You can volunteer for nursing at any time before you get your calling-up notice or direction.

Born in 1910 to 1919

Your age groups have already registered and most of you have been interviewed (see note on "What happens after registration?"). Some are being interviewed now. At your interview you will be given an opportunity of volunteering for one of the Services or you will be told what other kind of war work you will have to do. You may, if you wish, volunteer for any of these Services or war jobs, before interview, through an Employment Exchange (but if you are in work, read the section, "If you are in a job"). You will not have a free choice, but if possible you will be placed in the work you prefer.

You must be prepared to leave home unless this would mean exceptional hardship.

Born before 1910

Some of you have registered and others will be registering shortly.

If you have registered, look at the preceding section for "Women born in 1910 to 1919." It applies also to you.

If you have not registered you are free to volunteer at once for the Services or war industry (but if you are in work, see the section, "If you are in a job").

Born in 1922 and 1923

You will register with your age group but you do not need to wait for registration. You can volunteer now for the Services or nursing or for munition work. If you are in work, see the section, "If you are in a job."

Women with domestic responsibilities

You will be dealt with according to your age group, but if you have domestic responsibilities which make it impossible for you to take a job you will not be expected to do so. You may be asked to discuss your position with an independent women's panel. If you are directed to take a job you are able to appeal to an independent board.

THERE has been so much talk about women being called up for one thing and another, that you will probably want to know exactly how you stand. No matter whether you are 18 or 60, married or single — no matter whether you have children or not, or a husband in the Forces or not — you can find here exactly what is expected of you and how the various Government orders affect you.

What is registration?

Every British woman in Great Britain, whether married or single, has to go to a local office of the Ministry of Labour on the day that her age group is called and give certain facts about herself. (There are a few exceptions such as women already in the Women's Auxiliary Services This information is used by the Ministry of Labour to decide what women are available to go into war service.

Women born in the years 1908 to 1921 were registered by February 7th, 1942, and it has been announced that women born in 1907, 1906 and 1905 will register fortnightly beginning on February 21st.

What happens after registration?

Registration is normally followed by an interview.

The only women who are not called for interview are those with children of their own under 14 living with them, and those already in important work.

Everyone else is called for interview beginning with those who are not in jobs. Don't think that something has gone wrong if you are not called at once.

When you are interviewed (or whether you are interviewed at all) depends on the kind of work you are doing. Even though your present work may be important, you may be interviewed with a view to arranging for an older woman to take your place, releasing you for more active work.

Your employer is always consulted before you are called for interview.

What is compulsory service?

Compulsory service may take one of two forms :

1 — compulsory call-up to the Women's Auxiliary Services (commonly called conscription),

2 — compulsory call-up to work in industry (commonly called direction).

The compulsory call-up to the Women's Auxiliary Services applies only to single women and widows without children, and at present to those who were born in 1920 or 1921. But read the section dealing with these age groups . It may be extended to other age groups.

A *compulsory direction* requires a woman to go to any civilian job. If she disobeys it, she is liable to be prosecuted.

Volunteering

Whatever you are thinking of doing, whether volunteering for the Services or any war job, you should always consult the Employment Exchange first. A woman between 20 and 31 years of age must get her job through an Exchange. This is made compulsory under the Employment of Women (Control of Engagement) Order which came into force on February 16th. (There are some exceptions to this which the Exchange can tell you about).

If you are in a job

If a woman who is already in a job volunteers for the Women's Services or Civil Defence, the Exchange always asks her employer whether he wants to make a case for keeping her because of the importance of her present work. But it is only if her work is very important that the Exchange will refuse on these grounds her application to join up.

If your job is one covered by an Essential Work Order if it is, there will be a notice up where you work), you cannot leave it to volunteer, or for any other reason, without the permission of the National Service Officer of the Ministry of Labour.

If you do not know whether you should or may leave your present work, ask at your local Employment Exchange.

Appeals

If you are in the 1920 or 1921 age group being called up, you can appeal to an independent tribunal on grounds of conscience or exceptional hardship. If you are in the older age groups, you can appeal to an independent Board against your compulsory direction. You will be told how to do this by the local office of the Ministry of Labour at the right time.

Married Women
and Mothers of Young Children

Mothers of young children

You register with your age group, but if you have a child of your own under 14 living with you, you cannot be called up for the Women's Services and you will not even be asked to come for interview after registration.

You can volunteer, as so many of you already have done, for war work or Civil Defence. Or perhaps you could look after a neighbour's children during the day so that she could go into munition work. Or perhaps you could take in war workers as lodgers. Or, again, part-time work may be available in your district, either in a munition factory or in some other important work. For example, you might be able to work during the rush hours at a shop, thus releasing someone else to go full-time into a munition factory. You can find out whether part-time work of this sort is available by asking at your local Employment Exchange.

It will be a help if you look around to see what can be done, make your own arrangements, and then simply report to the Employment Exchange. You are free to seek the employment you prefer and make the arrangements direct with the employer, even if you are between 20 and 31.

Expectant Mothers

You must register with your age group, but you will not be asked to take up work.

Wives whose husbands are at home

You must register with your age group, but you cannot be called up into the Services: you are, however, free to volunteer if you are aged between 17½ and 43 (50 in the case of ex-service women).

After you have been registered, you will be interviewed and dealt with as single women of your age group are, with due regard to your domestic responsibilities, but you will *not* be asked to leave your home: you will be sent to work within daily travelling distance only. If you have not registered, see section under "Single Women," on "Women born before 1910."

Wives of Men in the Navy, Army, or Air Force, or the Merchant Navy

The same as for wives whose husbands are at home.

All other Married Women

You must register with your age group and what applies to single women in your age group applies to you, except that you cannot be called up for the Women's Services. You may of course volunteer for them, as so many of you have already done. Due regard will be paid to your domestic responsibilities.

Women who marry after joining the Services

If you marry after joining one of the Services you are still a member of the Force in which you are enrolled and you cannot leave without permission.

Widows

A widow who has no young children living with her is in the same position as a single woman in the same age group, except that the Ministry of Labour will pay special regard to the position of women recently widowed.

Cut this out and keep it

It is an official statement issued by the Ministry of Labour and National Service

---

Services and War Work for which women are wanted now

SERVICES	INDUSTRIAL WORK	
Women's Auxiliary Services	Munitions (including iron and steel, chemicals, radio, and electric cables)	Domestic work in hospitals, canteens and hostels for munitions and armament works
Civil Defence		
Nursing Services	Light alloys	
Women's Land Army	Timber production	Transport service, including maintenance
Navy, Army and Air Force Institutes	Post Office engineering	

Local jobs for those who cannot leave home to replace those who can

CONSCIENTIOUS OBJECTORS

Conscription began in May, 1939 when the Military Training Act was introduced for young men aged 20 and 21, who were required to undertake six months' military training. On the first day of the war, Parliament passed the National Services (Armed Forces) Act, making all men aged between 18 and 41 liable for conscription.

One of the interesting features of the Act was the provision for conscientious objection to military service on either pacifist or political grounds. When introducing the Act to Parliament, Neville Chamberlain had said, "Where scruples are conscientiously held we desire that they should be respected and that there should be no persecution of those who hold them."

When the 20 to 23 age group registered for military service on 21st October 1939, 22 in every 1,000 claimed their right of conscience and went before their respective local tribunals. The tribunals consisted of 5 members, one of whom had to be approved by the trade union, and, unlike the tribunals of the Great War, the War Office was not represented. The objector had the right of appeal to a higher tribunal.

After Dunkirk, public opinion swung sharply against objectors as invasion hysteria mounted. Of the 138 local authorities, 119 voted to dismiss or suspend for the duration all objectors in their service, 13 decided to reduce objectors' pay to that of private soldiers, and only 16 decided to take no action at all.

It was the many well-publicised reports of objectors showing conspicuous courage in bomb-disposal units or civil defence that helped to reduce the prejudice. Indeed, one of the first units ashore on D-Day, Parachute Field Ambulances, had scores of objectors in its ranks.

Of the 59,192 men and women who claimed conscientious objection only 3,577 were given unconditional exemption from war work. A further 28,720 were registered providing they took up approval work and 14,691 were registered for non-combat duties with the armed forces. The remaining 12,204 had their claims rejected and remained liable for call up for military service.

Keep mum she's not so dumb!

CARELESS TALK COSTS LIVES

The first tribunal for Conscientious Objectors held at Ruskin Chambers, Corporation Street, 27th July 1939.

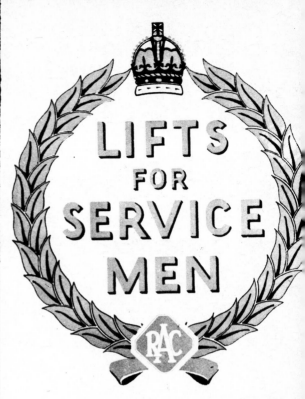

PUBLIC NOTICES JULY 29, 1942

CITY OF BIRMINGHAM

ENEMY INVASION

INSTRUCTIONS TO THE PUBLIC UNDER ENEMY INVASION CONDITIONS

The following Instructions are issued for the guidance of the public as to what they should do in the event of invasion:—

1. STAND FIRM. This means that as long as your normal occupation continues, you should remain at work. If the approach of the Enemy prevents your going to work and you have not been earmarked for any other task, LET THE LOCAL WARDEN KNOW that you are free to undertake duties which may be allotted to you; otherwise REMAIN AT YOUR HOME, KEEP CALM AND DO NOT LISTEN TO RUMOURS. Be patient if the obtaining of Food, &c., is a more difficult business than IT IS NORMALLY. Keep off the roads and keep indoors after dark. Keep your Gas Mask with you always—if enemy planes are overhead, keep under cover—if you do this no gas spray can hurt you—if the Gas Alarm is sounded wear your Gas Mask and you will be in no danger from Gas.

2. If you are a whole-time or part-time Civil Defence worker or have been earmarked for other essential duties THAT IS YOUR JOB IN INVASION. You will already have been notified as to what is required of you.

3. WHO FIGHTS THE ENEMY? The Military, which includes the Home Guard, are there to fight the enemy. If there are no military near where you are and isolated enemy parachute troops land near you, you are allowed by International Law to overcome them for the protection of your own home. Apart from this, you should leave the Military to fight the Enemy, and your job is to avoid hampering the Military by blocking the roads or by getting in between the enemy and our troops.

4. SHOULD I LEAVE MY HOME? If your Home is destroyed by Enemy action or is on fire, you should go quietly and quickly to a friend's or relative's house, or a public shelter or Rest Centre near by, where you will not impede the Military. You should think this problem out beforehand for yourself—THE ONE THING YOU MUST NOT DO IS TO PANIC AND BLOCK THE ROADS. An orderly move to a safer place from an area in which you cannot remain is quite different from an unorganised general movement.

5. FOOD AND WATER. Have enough in your house to enable you and your family to keep going for 48 hours in the event of normal supplies being temporarily dislocated.

6. DO NOT OBEY the order of unknown people to evacuate your home and go anywhere—this is a favourite FIFTH column trick—the Military, Police, Civil Defence personnel or Ministry of Information loud-speaker vans will tell you what to do. REMEMBER the enemy can impersonate such people, so be suspicious of any order which strikes you as wrong or of anyone spreading alarming information. Keep a suspect under observation until able to inform Police or Military.

7. DAMAGE TO YOUR OWN PROPERTY BY OUR OWN TROOPS. It is inevitable that houses, gardens, &c., MUST suffer some damage in the process of making defences. This you must accept.

IF YOU SEE ENEMY TROOPS. Tell the nearest Police Officer or Warden, but remember to be able to say WHERE you saw the enemy, WHEN, HOW MANY OF THEM, and WHICH WAY THEY WERE MOVING.

Issued by direction of the Birmingham Invasion Committee,

F. H. C. WILTSHIRE,
Town Clerk and Controller of Civil Defence.

July, 1942.

A Crusader tank on trials, June, 1940.

An anti-aircraft rocket battery opens up, July 1942.

HERR DOKTOR'S DILEMMA

Goebbels, in ' Das Reich,'' admits that Germany '' for the time being is receiving bitter wounds '' through the R.A.F.'s '' spiteful attacks.''

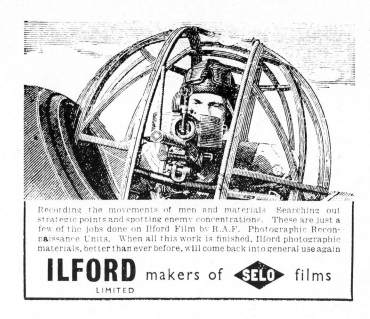

Left: RAF Balloon Barrage unit stationed at Ridgacre Road, Quinton, 1940.

In 1943 a man employed by the Air Ministry Directorate of Works discovered that the principal task given to a U.S. Army medical unit stationed near Birmingham was to analyse the city's food and drink to see if it was pure enough for American consumption. The research involved an official pub crawl on a grand scale, and the officer in charge of the unit reported "Mild was excellent for consumption by G.I.'s, bitter not so good although quite intoxicating in quantity, and bottled beer would do credit to the Borgias"!

The King visits a balloon centre, 19th April, 1940.

LUFTWAFFE INTELLIGENCE
FILES

During the summer of 1939 as Europe moved inexorably towards war, the Luftwaffe undertook a major photo-reconnaissance exercise of the British Isles. Priority was given to the location of possible industrial and communications targets rather than military installations.

Birmingham was located in target area BB23 along with Coventry, Darlaston, West Bromwich, Bromsgrove, Banbury, Leamington, Northampton, Market Harborough, Rugby and Stony Stratford (Militärgeographische Objektkarte Nr 8 Midlands). Individual factories, railway yards, tramway depots and so on were allocated target numbers and files containing any known information were collated. Contrary to popular myth, hospitals were clearly marked on target maps with large red crosses so that they would not be attacked in mistake for factories.

When Goering issued his directive to the Luftwaffe to attack Britain's vital war industries, Birmingham was named along with Coventry, Wolverhampton and Liverpool to receive special attention.

When the attacks on Birmingham began, the Luftwaffe's comprehensive photo-reconnaissance exercises had not been followed up by intelligence on the ground. Birmingham's industrial expansion before 1939 had taken place on the outskirts on the city — at Selly Oak, Northfield and Longbridge, where the largest and most modern factories could be found. Yet these targets were hardly hit. The Austin Motor Co. and Austin Aero Co. at Longbridge and Cofton Hackett were not bombed, even though German Intelligence believed that Spitfires were being built there, and were subjected to only one abortive daylight raid. Serck Radiators Ltd. in Warwick Road, Tyseley were never put out of action yet, during the Battle of Britain, they were the only manufacturers in the country of Spitfire and Hurricane radiators and oil coolers. Fort Dunlop, although hit several times, was never subjected to a concentrated attack, and S.U. Carburettors, our sole producer of aircraft carburettors, was not hit until November, 1940, by which time dispersal plans were already in operation.

The bombed central area of the city, although containing important plants such as Morris and B.S.A., also contained a large number of declining industries not essential to the war effort.

In only 4 raids were more than 100 houses destroyed, and in only 3 were more than 10 factories seriously damaged. Birmingham Civil Defence reports that a total of 5,129 HE bombs were dropped on the city, of which 930 failed to detonate, approximately 1 HE bomb for every 10 acres of the city's area.

German records give the following payloads dropped on Birmingham. For the whole of October 1940, 217 tons HE and 591 canisters of incendiaries, for the night of the 25th November, 227 tons HE and 457 canisters of incendiaries, and for the whole of December 409 tons of HE and 1,313 canisters of incendiaries. By March, 1941, when the bulk of the Luftwaffe was being withdrawn for operations against the Soviet Union, the tonnage was down to 120 tons HE for the whole month.

GB **8.** BB 23, Nr. 80: Maschinenfabrik Word in Birmingham (Warwickshire).
Blick auf Verwaltungsgebäude und Werkhallen der Maschinenfabrik von H. W. Word & Co. Ltd. in der Drale Road. Selly Oak.

GB 8, BB 23, Nr. 17: Automobilfabrik Morris Commercial Car's in Birmingham (Warwickshire).
Herstellung von Kraftwagen und Zubehör. Nahe der Adderley Park Station, Birmingham-Ost.

GB 8, BB 23, Nr. 79: Automobilfabrik Wolseley Works Ltd. in Birmingham (Warwickshire).
Herstellung von Kraftwagen und Zubehör.

GB 8, BB 23, Nr. 5: Großkraftwerk Hams Hall in Birmingham (Warwickshire).
Elektrizitätswerk "Hams Hall, Nechells Prince's Station", Hochspannung: 11, 22, 33 kV; Höchstlast: 512 136 kW;
Generatorgesamtleistung: 396 250 kW; Umformer, Gleichricht-Gesamtleistung: 95 822 kW.

Birmingham-W
Rootes u. Co. Ltd. Flugzeugzellenfabrik

GB 7418 b
Nur für den Dienstgebrauch

Kriegsaufnahme:
608 R 53

Länge (westl. Greenw.): 2° 0' 15''   Breite: 52° 30' 18'' (Blattmitte)
Mißweisung: — 11° 55' (Mitte 1938)

Maßstab etwa 1:15 300

ⓒ GB 7418 Rootes u. Co. Ltd. Flugzeugzellenfabrik
ⓐ GB 7057 Albion-Eisenwerk Agruppe + Werken
ⓑ GB 7111 Birmingham Aluminium Castings Co.Ltd. Aluminium-fabrik

Genst. 5. Abt. Oktober 1940
Karte 1:100 000
GB 23

Birmingham-Tyseley
Werk für Motorenteile Hay Hall Works

GB 732 b
Nur für den Dienstgebrauch

Bild Nr. 468 L 53/55
Aufnahme vom 8.9.39

Länge (westl. Greenw.): 1° 50' 10''   Breite: 52° 27' 30''
Mißweisung: —11° 31' (Mitte 1940)   Zielhöhe über NN 120 m

Maßstab etwa 1:14 500

ⓐ G.B.732 Werk für Motorenteile Hay Hall Works
ⓑ G.B.804 Werk für Motorenteile Singer Works
ⓒ G.B.736 Werk für Motorenteile Rover Motor Works
ⓓ G.B.7823 Waffenfabrik Small-Arms Factory
ⓔ G.B.401 Güter-Bahnhof
ⓕ G.B.681 Rüstungsfabrik Joseph Lucas Ltd. Werk Formans Road
ⓖ G.B.8218 Rüstungsfabrik Joseph Lucas Ltd. Werk Shaftmoor Lane

72

Birmingham

Werk für Motorenteile und Aluminiumguß Aluminium Casting Co.

GB 733 c

Nur für den Dienstgebrauch

n. Bild Nr. 468 L 32

Länge (westl. Greenw.): 1° 49′ 25″   Breite: 52° 30′ 40″
Mißweisung: —11° 31′ (Mitte 1940)   Zielhöhe über NN 95 m

Maßstab 1:10 560

GB 733 Werk für Motorenteile und Aluminiumguß Aluminium Casting Co.

1) Fabrikations- und Montagehallen   etwa 44 000 qm
2) Verwaltungsgebäude   etwa 3 300 qm
                                             etwa 47 300 qm
   bebaute Fläche (Schwerpunkt)
   Gesamtausdehnung   etwa 338 000 qm
   Gleisanschluß nicht vorhanden

Birmingham

Werk für Motorenteile Singer Works

GB 804 c

Nur für den Dienstgebrauch

n. Bild Nr. 468 L 54

Länge (westl. Greenw.): 1° 50′ 40″   Breite: 52° 27′ 45″
Mißweisung: —11° 31′ (Mitte 1940)   Zielhöhe über NN 125 m

Maßstab 1:10 560

GB 804 Werk für Motorenteile Singer Works

1) Werkhallen   etwa 22 000 qm
2) Verwaltungsgebäude   etwa 5 500 qm
3) Lagergebäude u. Schuppen   etwa 2 500 qm
                                      etwa 30 000 qm
   bebaute Fläche (Schwerpunkt)
   Gesamtausdehnung   etwa 150 000 qm

AY JONES:

When I got off the train at Snow Hill Station, after a trip to Wales, a workman offered to carry my large suitcase. When I told him that I lived in Ryland Road he said that he was very sorry to tell me that all the houses in our road had just been totally demolished by a landmine. Knowing my family would have been there at the time I grew more and more terrified as I approached the area. As I got to the bottom of Ryland Road I saw that all the houses were still intact, but Upper Ryland Road had been completely flattened."

Holliday Street.

Air Raid After Care Rest Centres

Members of the public are again reminded of the advice of the Minister of Health, that if they are rendered homeless by air raids, and have relatives or friends within easy reach, they should go to them. Advance arrangements with friends or relatives for mutual assistance should be made.

Billeting allowances at the rate of 5/- per week for each adult, and 3/- per week for each child under 14 will be payable to the householders providing the accommodation for a period of 14 days.

If you are compelled to leave your home as a result of enemy action, and have no alternative accommodation, you should proceed immediately after an air raid to the nearest Rest Centre, the addresses of which are as follows :—

*78, Cornwall Street, 3.
Birmingham Settlement, Summer Lane, 19.
Hope Street Schools, Gooch Street, 5.
Summer Lane Schools, 19.
Grosvenor Street Schools, 5.
*Digbeth Institute, Digbeth, 5.
Friends' Institute, 220, Moseley Road, 12.
Upper Highgate Street Schools, Moseley Road, 12.
*St. Paul's Church Rooms, St. Paul's Road, 12.
Dennis Road Schools, Balsall Heath, 12.
*St. John's Schools, Ivor Road, Sparkhill, 11.
Formans Road Schools, Sparkhill, 11.
College Road Schools, Moseley, 13.
*Methodist Schools, Coventry Road (opposite Jenkins Street), 10.
Marlborough Road Schools, Small Heath, 10.
Oakley Road Schools, Small Heath, 10.
St. Benedict's Road Schools, Small Heath, 10.
Conway Road Schools, Sparkbrook, 11.
*Friends' Institute, Berkeley Road, Hay Mills, 25.
Church Road Schools, Yardley, 25.
Bierton Road Schools, Yardley, 25.
*Y.W.C.A., Richmond Road, Stechford, 25.
Alston Road Schools, 9.
Tilton Road Schools, Small Heath, 9.
*Birmingham Medical Mission, Kitts Green Road, Lea Hall, 26.
Cockshut Hill Schools, Yardley, 26.
Silvermere Road Schools, Sheldon, 26.
Lea Village Schools, Yardley, 26.
*Baptist Schools, Heneage Street, 7.
Charles Arthur Street Schools, 7.
Bloomsbury Schools, Lingard Street, 7.
*Methodist Schools, Victoria Road, 6. (Entrance Lichfield Road).
Vicarage Road Schools, Aston, 6.
*Methodist Schools, Mansfield Road, Aston, 6.
St. Mary's Mission Room, Hutton Road, Handsworth, 20.

Canterbury Road Schools, Handsworth, 20.
Lozells Street Schools, 19.
Albert Road Schools, Aston, 6.
*Methodist Schools, Rookery Road, Handsworth, 21.
Rookery Road Schools, Handsworth, 21.
*Methodist Schools, Hockley Street, 18.
Burbury Street Schools, Farm Street, 19.
*Vestry Hall, Islington Row, 15.
Y.W.C.A. Social Service Centre, 67, Broad Street, 1.
Church of the Redeemer School Room, Hagley Road, 16.
Islington Methodist Church Institute, St. Martin's Street, 15.
*Baptist Schools, High Street, Harborne, 17.
Station Road School, Harborne, 17.
*Methodist School Rooms, College Road, Quinton, 32.
Four Dwellings Schools, Quinton, 32.
*The Institute, Church Road, Northfield, 31.
Tinker's Farm Road Schools, Northfield, 31.
Turves Green Schools, 31.
Ruberv Schools, Bristol Road South.
*Community Hall, Weoley Castle, 29.
Ilmington Road Schools, 29.
*The Institute, Hazelwell Street, 30.
Friends' Hall, Watford Road, King's Norton, 30.
Colmore Road Schools, King's Heath, 14.
Cotteridge Schools, Pershore Road, 30.
*The Institute, 648, Bristol Road, 29.
St. Stephen's Church Hall, Pershore Road, Selly Park, 29.
Bournville Schools, Linden Road, 30.
*Baptist Schools, Alexander Road, 27.
Pitmaston Road Schools, Hall Green, 28.
Acocks Green Schools, Warwick Road, 27.
*Community Hall, Yardley Wood Road, 14.
Billesley Schools, Trittiford Road, 14.
Yardley Wood Schools, 14.
*St. Mark's Rooms, Washwood Heath Road, 8.
Nansen Road Schools, Saltley, 8.

ALWAYS CARRY YOUR GAS MASK

Fazeley Street Canal, 1st November 1940.

REG HANDLEY (Cadbury's senior warehouse foreman):
"It was decided to transfer the wages department down into the basement for safety reasons, but when the bomb hit the centre of the bridge carrying the canal over Bournville Lane, it caused part of the section to be flooded. I can remember seeing pound notes floating everywhere." December, 1940.

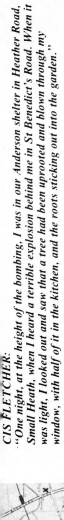

CIS FLETCHER:

"One night, at the height of the bombing, I was in our Anderson shelter in Heather Road, Small Heath, when I heard a terrible explosion behind me in St Benedict's Road. When it was light, I looked out and saw that a tree had been uprooted and blown through my window, with half of it in the kitchen, and the roots sticking out into the garden."

An Anderson Shelter blown over the rooftops into Avenue Road, Aston, May, 1941.

Alfred Road, Sparkbrook, 2nd January 1941.

Birmingham, 19th November 1940

The black dots show where German high explosive bombs fell (or serious fires started) on the night of Tuesday 19th November 1940. Unexploded or delayed action bombs are marked "X".

This was Birmingham's 50th air raid and one of the heaviest. The warning siren sounded at 18.50 hrs. and the all clear at 04.29 hrs. the following morning.

Casualties were about 1500 killed and injured.

John Whybrow Collection, Sparkbrook, Birmingham.
By courtesy of the City of Birmingham.
Enclosed with John Whybrow's Newsletter, February 1975.

Bromford Lane, Erdington.

Hodge Hill Common.

*Vincent Street, Balsall
Heath, 29th October 1940*

*The Carlton Cinema,
Taunton Road, Sparkhill,
25th October 1940.*

SHELTERS

Anderson Shelters

The Anderson shelter(named after Sir John Anderson, Secretary of State for Home Affairs and Home Security) became a familiar sight at the bottom of many a garden. Cheap to produce, the Anderson consisted of two curved corrugated steel walls which met in a ridge at the top and were then bolted to sturdy rails to give the structure strength. The Anderson was then planted 3 feet into the ground and covered with at least 18 inches of soil. The entrance was protected by a steel shield and a blast wall made of soil. Though very effective and capable of protecting up to 6 people from almost anything but a direct hit, Andersons were prone to flooding and early models were too small to sleep in. Approximately 2,250,000 were distributed free of charge by the Government, but in October, 1939, people earning over £5 a week had to buy their own for prices ranging from £6.14s to £10 18s each. Production ceased in March, 1940 due to the shortage of steel and a change in Government policy that favoured the building of communal shelters.

Morrison shelters

Named after the Minister of Home Security, Herbert Morrison, the Morrison shelter, like the Anderson, was designed for family use. Morrisons were unique in that they could be erected indoors. Essentially the Morrison looked like a steel table, standing 2 feet 9 inches high with sides of wire mesh. Issued free to most people, some 500,000 were in use by November, 1941.

Trench Shelters

Many trench shelters were excavated in public parks during the Munich crisis of 1938. At the beginning of the war, the Government ordered local authorities to make these shelters more permanent by lining the sides and roofing them with concrete or steel. These shelters were unpopular and were often impossible to keep waterproof.

Surface Shelters

Introduced in March, 1940, these were "communal" shelters designed to protect up to 50 residents from a single street and were built from brick and concrete. However, many early shelters of this type were built without mortar because of a cement shortage and were prone to collapse from bomb blast. Ventilation was limited and even when chemical toilets were provided they stank. All in all they were not very popular.

Public Shelters

Surveys were undertaken in town centres to assess how many existing cellars and vaults could be used as public shelters. Also brick and concrete public shelters, such as the one constructed in the Old Square (by Lewis's), were specially built. Shelters of this type gained individual characteristics and some sort of social life developed with official support, with concerts, play reading, libraries, sing songs, and so on. The large public shelters had full-time "shelter wardens" and first aid posts.

People saved by a Morrison Shelter. Highgate Road, Sparkbroo. 30th July 1942.

A public shelter.

Trench shelters.

BRUMMIES ABROAD

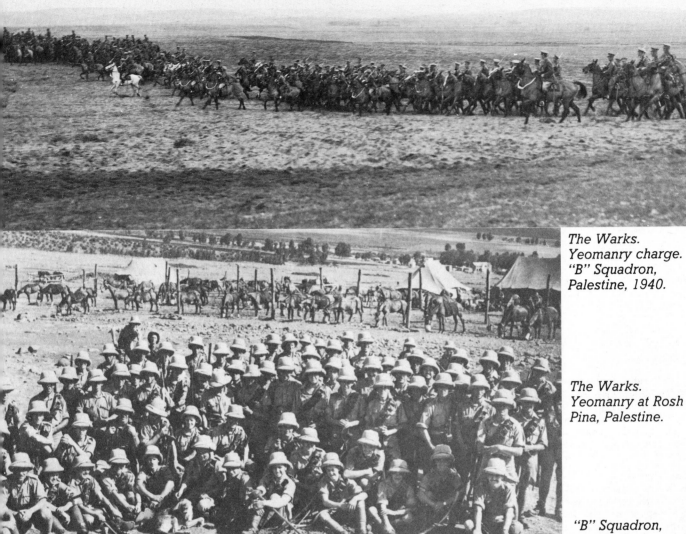

The Warks.
Yeomanry charge.
"B" Squadron,
Palestine, 1940.

The Warks.
Yeomanry at Rosh
Pina, Palestine.

"B" Squadron,
Warks, Yeomanry,
near Beirut, 1943.

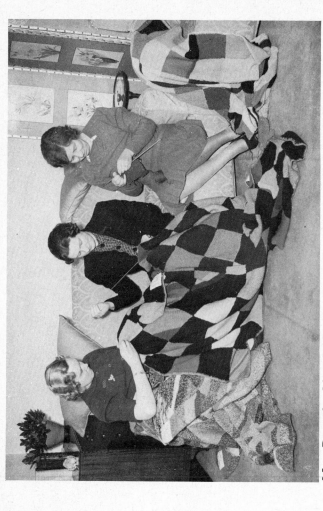

Mrs. Dorothy Lloyd, Neville Chamberlain's daughter, (centre) and friends, at her home in Calthorpe Road, Edgbaston, take part in the Army Blanket Scheme, 1940.

Mrs Neville Chamberlain and the Earl of Clarendon inspect parcels of food and medical supplies before their dispatch to

84

The Bull Ring Club - Birmingham P.O.W.'s at their camp in Germany.

DOUGLAS PREATOR (of Winson Green Road):
"Although I was in the Welsh Guards, in our particluar intake (23rd December 1939) there were a great many Brummies.
I was captured at Boulogne in 1940 and held by the Germans until 1945. These photographs were taken during my 'stay' at Reigesfeld."

Entertainment at Reigesfeld P.O.W. Camp, Germany.

The funeral of a P.O.W., ironically killed by an American bomb which fell short of its target, Reigesfeld P.O.W. Camp, Germany.

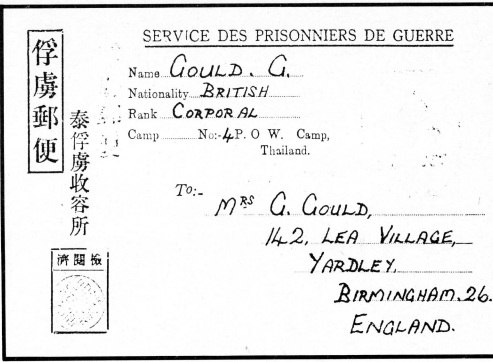

俘虜郵便

泰俘虜收容所

濟閱檢

SERVICE DES PRISONNIERS DE GUERRE

Name GOULD. G.
Nationality BRITISH
Rank CORPORAL
Camp No:-4 P. O W. Camp,
Thailand.

To:-

Mrs G. GOULD,
142, LEA VILLAGE,
YARDLEY,
BIRMINGHAM. 26.
ENGLAND.

IMPERIAL JAPANESE ARMY

Date 10TH JUNE 1944

Your mails (and ———) are received with thanks.
My health is (good, usual, poor).
I am ill in hospital.
I am working for pay (I am paid monthly salary).
I am not working.
My best regards to YOURSELF, GILLEAN, MOM, DAD, AMY, STAN,
VIC, HILDA, AND ALL AT 202, CHURCHILL RD.

Yours ever,

George.

*Right: Only 6 Midlanders
survived the torpedo attack and
George Gould (left) was the sole
survivor from Birmingham. An
American base, Taipan,
September, 1944.*

CAPTAIN KENNETH CRISP-JONES, R.A.S.C. (now Major):
"I was attached to the District Commissioner at Fort Hall, Kenya, and on VE Day I was detailed to go to an out-station at Kananga (later the centre of Mau Mau activities) to read the proclamation that war was over.
Whoever would have thought that I, a lad from Upland Road, Selly Park, would one day represent my King in a far-off country!"

HARRY MULLOY (300th Battery 98th Heavy A.A. Regt.):
"In March, 1945 we entered Wilhelmshaven in Germany. The children used to wait outside the camp gates for food and chocolate. I befriended a starving German family, much against the fraternisation rules, and managed to smuggle out rations from the cookhouse and then take them round to them. Even to this day we still correspond.
I hitch-hiked back to Holland to join in the victory celebrations."

Right: VE day, Harlingen, Holland.

I feel I cannot let you leave 21 Army Group on your return to civil life without a message of thanks and farewell. Together we have carried through one of the most successful campaigns in history, and it has been our good fortune to be members of this great team. God Bless you and God speed.

B. L. Montgomery

**FIELD MARSHAL
COMMANDER IN CHIEF**

BAOR·1945

89

WAR BRIDES

Because of the great influx of soldiers of different nationalities into the area, it was inevitable that many local girls would meet them, fall in love and eventually marry.

In January, 1946, 450 British wives of American Servicemen and 170 babies left England on the liner "Argentina". Upon their arrival in New York they were met by the yacht "Miss America". A band, on board the yacht, did not play as many of the babies were still asleep, but as soon as the liner docked a rousing "Here comes the Bride" welcomed the new arrivals ashore. In February, after being delayed by a 65 m.p.h. gale for 24 hours, the "Queen Mary" left Southampton with 2,334 wives and children to start their new lives in America.

Many other girls moved to Canada (in a survey, carried out in December 1946, the total number of U.K. dependants recorded as 44,886 wives and 21,358 children), Australia and South Africa, but it was not always a story of departures as quite a few overseas servicemen liked Birmingham so much that they stayed here, with their new wives, after they were demobbed.

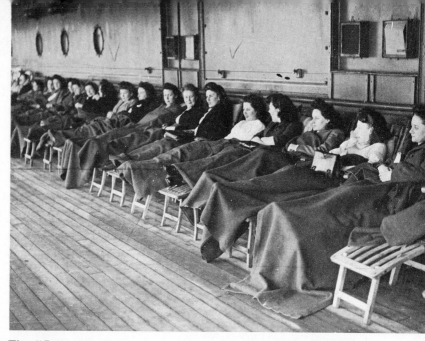

The "Argentina" leaves Southampton bound for the U.S.

Below: the "Marine Jumper" en route for the U.S. Mrs Dorothy Toombs of Birmingham (left) is off to join her husband Raymond.

MARGARET DOGGETT:
"The American soldiers at Beakes Road were confined to their barracks because D-Day was imminent, but my sisiter-in-law Olive's fiancé Master Sgt. Walter Lindberg was allowed a 24-hour pass for their wedding, on 3rd June 1944, and his friends were given permission to attend the reception itself." (Below)

Mrs Horber of Edgbaston and Mrs. Choute of Weoley Castle stroll along the deck of the "Queen Mary".

HILDA MINSHALL:
"I lived in Warren Road, Stirchley, and met my future husband Henry, who was British born, while he was over here with the Royal Canadian Artillery. We were married at Stirchley 'Church of the Ascension', 25th May 1940. Henry returned to Canada in 1945 for his demob and I sailed out to join him the following year on the 'Aquitania', which was known as 'the war brides ship'. However we decided we preferred Brum and came back here in 1947."

Below: The "Church of Our Lady of the Rosary", Saltley, 19th May 1945. The wedding of Henry and Hilda Mleczko. Hilda, from Alum Rock, and her Polish-Canadian husband now live in Glace Bay, Nova Scotia.

THE WARTIME LORD MAYORS

Right: James Crump, (1938-39), at the Civic Service in St Martin's Church, October 1939, with Dr. W. C. Barnes, Bishop of Birmingham, Dr. Raymond Priestley, Vice-Chancellor of the University and Canon Guy Rogers.

Below: Theodore Pritchett, (1939-40), at the Prince of Wales charity performance, 7th April 1940, with Emile Littler, the Lady Mayoress and Arthur Askey.

Wilfrid Martineau, (1940-41), inspects the Birmingham Air Training Corps Guard, 5th May 1941.

Norman Tiptaft, (1941-42) with 4 Birmingham soldiers.

Walter Lewis, (1942-43), with his wife and daughter, Joyce.

Left: Lionel Aldridge, (1943-44), with "Nye" Bevan, Minister of Health, on the left.

Below: William Wiggins-Davies, (1944-45) meets the workers, 4th May 1945.

The Birmingham Mail

LIGHTING-UP TIME, 10.43 p.m.

Nº. 24,700

MONDAY, MAY 7, 1945

ONE PENNY

GERMANS ANNOUNCE SURRENDER

All Fighting Troops Lay Down Their Arms

THE NATION'S LEADER

Patton's Men Within 15 Miles of Prague

PATRIOTS SAID TO HAVE SURROUNDED CITY

General Patton's U.S. Third Army columns, racing into Czecho-Slovakia in response to the patriot call for help, to-day advanced to within 15 miles of Prague, from which

THIS is the great day. The war in Europe is over, Germany has surrendered unconditionally.

The news for which we have all been so anxiously waiting was broadcast by the German Foreign Minister shortly after 2 o'clock to-day. He said: "German men and women: The High Command of the armed forces has to-day, at the order of Grand-Admiral Doenitz, declared the unconditional surrender of all fighting German troops."

Thus ends the conflict which began on that Sunday morning in September, 1939—five years, eight months and four days ago—a conflict which has proved the most terrible, the most costly and the most destructive in history.

Our rejoicing to-day is tempered by the knowledge that the war in the Far East has still to be brought to a victorious end and that the resettlement and rebuilding of a new Europe will present problems of the first magnitude.

But for to-day, let us just remember that we have surmounted the greatest peril in our history, that we have played a worthy part in crushing the most appalling tyranny that has ever walked the earth — and as we rejoice let us have in mind the hundreds of thousands who have made the great sacrifice that we might live.

ADMIRAL DOENITZ GIVES THE ORDER

Admiral Doenitz who, on May 1, took over Hitler's powers, has been generally regarded as the man from whom surrender orders would go out to the last remaining German troops in arms. It was Doenitz who told the German people of Hitler's death. He claimed that Hitler had appointed him as his successor on the previous day.

The Danish home service radio stated shortly before 1.30 p.m. to-day: "It has just been announced that the German forces in Norway have

Nearly Six Years

PRINCIPAL EVENTS RECALLED

Sept. 1.—Hitler invades Poland.
Sept. 3.—Britain and France declare war.
Sept. 6.—French troops enter Germany.
Sept. 11.—British troops in France.
Sept. 17.—Russia invades Poland and the Polish defence practically collapses.
Nov. 8.—Bomb explosion in Munich beer cellar just after Hitler had left Nazi celebrations.
Nov. 30.—Russia attacks Finland.
Dec. 13.—Graf Spee chased into River Plate, where she is scuttled by Germans; Captain Langsdorff committed suicide.

1940

March. 12.—Peace treaty between Russia and Finland ceding Karelian Isthmus to Russia.
April 9.—Germans invade Denmark and Norway.
May 2.—British troops withdrawn from Norway after heavy fighting.
May 10.—Germans invaded Holland, Belgium and Luxembourg. Mr. Churchill becomes Premier.
May 15.—Germans break through on the Meuse.
May 28.—King Leopold of Belgium surrenders.
May 30.—B.E.F. evacuated through Dunkirk.
June 10.—Italy declares war on Great Britain and France.
June 22.—France surrenders.
Aug. 11.—Battle of Britain begun.
Aug. 15.—The day the Nazis had said they would be in London. Our airmen shoot down 180 German planes.
Aug. 24.—Defeated in the Battle of Britain, the Germans bomb London by night for the first time.
Sept. 1.—U.S. lease naval and air bases in return for 50 destroyers.
Sept. 17.—Italians advance on Egypt and occupy Sidi Barrani.
Nov. 11.—Fleet Air Arm cripples Italian Fleet. Fire raid on London.

May 12.—Von Arnim surrenders and North Africa is conquered.
June 11.—Pantellaria surrenders.
July 10.—Allies invade Sicily.
July 18.—Rome bombed.
July 22.—Americans capture Palermo.
July 25.—Mussolini deposed.
Aug. 5.—Eighth Army captures Catania.
Aug. 5.—Russians capture Orel.
Aug. 14.—Russians open Smolensk offensive.
Aug. 17.—Sicily conquered.
Sept. 3.—Italy invaded.
Sept. 8.—Italy surrendered to Allies.
Sept. 9.—Allied forces landed near Naples.

1940

Sept. 10.—Italian Fleet reached Malta. Rome occupied by German troops.
Sept. 12.—Liberation of Mussolini announced.
Sept. 25.—Capture of Smolensk and Roslavl by Russians announced.
Sept. 26.—U.S. forces landed on Mono Island (Solomons).
Oct. 1.—Naples occupied by Fifth Army.
Oct. 13.—Italy declared war on Germany.
Nov. 22.—Heaviest R.A.F. raid on Berlin to date; again on 23rd, 24th and 25th (by Mosquitoes), 26th, Nov. 28.—Teheran Conference (Marshal Stalin, President Roosevelt, Mr. Churchill. Ended on Dec. 1.
Dec. 2.—Berlin raided by R.A.F.; again on December 16, 23 and 29.

1944

Jan. 1.—Berlin raided again; also on 21st, 27th, 28th and 30th.
Jan. 4.—Russians back in Poland.
Jan. 6.—Fifth Army resume offensive.
Jan. 22.—New landing in Italy, on Anzio beach-head.
Jan. 24.—Anzio beach-head.
Jan. 25.—Anzio beach-head enlarged.
Feb. 14.—Cassino Monastery bombed.
Feb. 15.—Heavy respond on Berlin: 2,500 tons of bombs.
Feb. 18.—Fire raid on London.

The Birmingham Post

No. 27,074 1 4 TUESDAY, MAY 8, 1945 POSTAGE: INLAND 1½d. ONE PENNY

"VE" DAY TO-DAY: PREMIER'S 3 p.m. BROADCAST

THE KING WILL SPEAK TO EMPIRE AT 9 p.m.

ARMY CHIEFS ALSO TO BE HEARD

NAZIS IN EAST FLOUT SURRENDER ORDER

To-day is "VE" Day. At 3 p.m. Mr. Churchill will broadcast the news that the war in Europe is at an end, and at 9 p.m. there will be a broadcast by the King.

This was officially announced last night, at the end of a day of surprises and disappointments, in the following statement issued by the Ministry of Information:—

"It is understood that, in accordance with arrangements between the three Great Powers, an official announcement will be broadcast by the Prime Minister at three o'clock to-morrow afternoon, May 8.

"In view of this fact to-morrow (Tuesday) will be treated as Victory in Europe Day, and will be regarded as a holiday. The day following (Wednesday), May 9, will also be a holiday.

"H.M. the King will broadcast to the peoples of the British Empire and Commonwealth to-morrow (Tuesday) at 9 p.m. (D.B.S.T.). Parliament will meet at the usual time to-morrow."

It is also understood that there will be broadcasts to-day by General Eisenhower, Field-Marshal Montgomery and Field-Marshal Alexander.

The Germans had announced early yesterday afternoon that Grand Admiral Dönitz had unconditionally surrendered all German fighting forces; and the whole world eagerly awaited confirmation from the Allied leaders. Crowds gathered in the streets, flags were unfurled and there was singing and dancing.

In less than two hours after the German announcement, the Generals commanding the Nazi forces in Czechoslovakia, believed to be headed by Kesselring, flatly refused to follow their new Führer; and, in a broadcast from Prague, declared their intention to fight on.

This it was thought might have caused an alteration in

FIGHT CONTINUES IN PRAGUE

PATRIOTS HOLDING PART OF CITY

PATTON ADVANCING FROM PILSEN

The situation in Prague is not clear. Part of the city appears to be in the hands of Patriots, but German-controlled radio has stated that the struggle will be continued until the "Germans in the East are saved."

Meanwhile, General Patton's armour is reported seven miles from the city, and Red Army forces under Marshals Malinovsky and Eremenko are reported to be within a few miles of linking up east of Prague.

Marshal Eremenko's troops west and south-west of Moravska-Ostrava captured the towns of Freudenthal, Friedland (on the River Morava), Mahrisch Neustadt, Stepenov and a number of other places yesterday, according to last night's Soviet communiqué.

The Patriot Prague radio said at 11.36 last night that advanced United States tank units had just passed the town of Reporyje, about seven miles south of Prague. The situation appears to be that the Patriots hold the city but are surrounded by hostile German forces. It is also reported, however, that these Germans are themselves surrounded by advanced Russian columns.

The German-controlled Prague radio went off the air at 5.25 last evening and has not been heard since. It was this radio that denied that the German unconditional surrender, announced by Schwerin von Krosigk, referred to the Germans on the Russian front.

Germans Refuse to Surrender

The denial was contained in an order issued by the commander of the German troops in Czechoslovakia, which said:—

The report broadcast at mid-day to-day by the enemy station at Flensburg, saying that the Reich Government has capitulated unconditionally to the Soviet Union as well, does not correspond to facts. It is clearly enemy propaganda, intent on breaking our

Thanksgiving Day

To-day is Britain's real day of thanksgiving. Circumstances prevented yesterday that mere outburst of rejoicing which many had expected and more, many more, had feared. Circumstances, again, may delay till to-morrow any formal and organised expression of the nation's gratitude for a happy issue out of most of its afflictions. Spiritually, though, to-day is thanksgiving day.

To whom do we offer our thanks? First and foremost, to that Divine Providence which twice came to Britain's aid—in 1940, when a whole-hearted German attack might have caused us to suffer the fate of Holland and Belgium and France; in 1941, when the enemy's "second wind" strength, so to say, was divided unequally between Russia and ourselves. Is there anything, apart from this Divine Providence, to explain such signal errors of judgment?

Second, to the great leader who inspired us, in those dark days of 1940, to resist resolutely and with good spirit attacks immensely formidable even though not whole-hearted; who restrained us, too, when the tide had turned, from that raw haste in attack which might well have postponed victory beyond the world's capacity for endurance.

Third, to the fighting men of the R.A.F. who won the Battle of Britain; to the Royal Navy and the Merchant Navy, who shielded us and fed us; to the soldiers who, after the one great set-back in France, set themselves to the grim task of holding on and later to the almost incredibly difficult business of attack on a hostile Continent; to the patient, long-enduring victims of almost continuous air bombardment.

Fourth, to our Allies—and, in particular, to the Americans, who aided us long before formally they went to war; to the Russians who took, what we never had to take, the full shock of what was then the most powerful army the world had ever known.

Gratitude has its obligations. None of us forgets them, none of us will ignore them. For the moment, it is enough to "resolve highly" that all our debts shall be paid in full.

LONDON LETTER

Formalities of Capitulation

88, FLEET STREET, E.C. 4
Monday Night

Germany has capitulated; but the official announcement by the three chief Allied leaders of the end of hostilities in Europe has been deferred until the instrument of surrender has been signed and certain other formalities completed. That will be to-morrow, which, as to-night's official announcement says, will be "VE" Day, though after the scenes of the last few hours it must come as an anti-climax.

The Prime Minister, President Truman and Marshal Stalin will give the news simultaneously in the three Capitals, but by to-morrow afternoon it will sound belated. Mr. Churchill

was on an Irish business house, where the flag of Eire was hanging alongside the Union Jack.

New Wallpapers

The exhibition of historical and British wallpapers I mentioned some days ago was opened in the Suffolk Street Galleries to-day and will remain in London until the end of the month, when it will be taken to Manchester and Glasgow. It is a really good display. To the all-important question "when?", leading manufacturers replied that they could start production within twenty-four hours of receiving supplies of paper. They do not anticipate any difficulty over colours. The Board of

BURMA ADVANCE HAMPERED

PRE-MONSOON RAIN MENACE

MOPPING UP IN RANGOON

While British and Indian troops of the Fourteenth Army are mopping up in Rangoon, other Fourteenth Army men are finding their advance south towards the Burmese capital delayed by heavy pre-monsoon rain.

Japanese trapped in the territory east of the Irrawaddy are trying to escape through this Allied line along rough bullock tracks which cross the Pegu Yomas range.

In the Irrawaddy sector, Paungde, thirty-six miles south of Prome and 142 miles north-east of Rangoon, has been captured. In the oil region west of the Irrawaddy, Allied troops have captured guns and equipment in a fight at Yenanma, twenty-seven miles south of Minbu.

Road Blocks

On the West African Division front near the Arakan coast, Allied troops, advancing eastwards from Taungup, have encountered road blocks ten miles from Taungup on the way to the captured Irrawaddy town of Prome.

Major C. Tooke, of Ealing, is now faced with the task of restoring order in Rangoon after the orgy of looting which followed the departure of the Japanese. The whole fabric of civic life, already weakened by Japanese rule, broke down completely before the arrival of the British.

The so-called Burma Defence Army, consisting mainly of Burmans who switched over to the Japanese after the invasion of Burma and have now switched again, constitute the greatest potential threat to civil order in the country.

THE FAR EAST CAMPAIGN

"THE BIRMINGHAM POST" SPECIAL ARTICLES

With the close of the European War, that in the Far East is likely to get the attention it has long deserved.

Mr. H. M. Raleigh has left by air, for a tour of the Pacific fronts, as correspondent of "The Birmingham Post." He hopes, apart from his general work, to visit units with local associations.

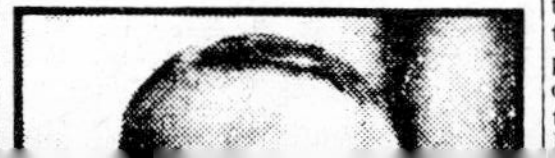

"THANK GOD" KEYNOTE OF BIRMINGHAM REACTION

LORD MAYOR'S ADVICE TO CELEBRATE VICTORY WORTHILY

TRIBUTE TO BRITAIN'S FIGHT FOR LIBERTY

"Thank God" is the keynote of messages from leaders of public life in Birmingham, marking the end of the war against Germany.

Mingled with tributes to the gallantry of the Forces is a profound gratitude for the great sacrifices made by the people, and an urgent resolve to build a happy future. Here are the messages:—

THE LORD MAYOR OF BIRMINGHAM:

The great moment is here. The swift, significant events of recent days detract nothing from its greatness, from our profound sense of relief, nor from our proud recognition of the gallantry of every fighting man in the British Navy, Army and Air Force, and in the fighting Services of our gallant Allies.

I say with all reverence and rejoicing: Thank God.

On this day of days, let each one of us give thanks either at our usual or nearest place of worship, or in our own home, or at our work.

I am proud of Birmingham and its citizens. The city has known many dark and anxious days and thousands have lost their loved ones; we think of them specially at this moment. Thousands of us still have our loved ones away, many still in danger or as prisoners of war.

Gift of Freedom

May God grant us true understanding of this, His supreme gift—the gift of freedom. I hope we can keep the clear knowledge of it throughout our lives and, to our little utmost, help build that better world which can be made, given less selfishness on all our parts.

We will do well to heed the recent words of our Prime Minister and rejoice soberly, conscious of the great task still ahead. The citizens of a city which, in its workshops, offices and services, has played so great a part in the achievement of this long-sought victory, need no call from me to celebrate that victory thankfully, cheerfully and worthily.

THE BISHOP OF BIRMINGHAM:

Thank God, fighting in the West has ceased. We can go forward with hope. At home we can now begin to rebuild our social life. Between the nations reason can begin to prevail over passion. Stern and difficult times lie ahead. We grieve that bloodshed continues in the Far East, but we now have the first ...

thousands who have generously given their lives that we may live. For the future we ask the help of God to finish the war and to establish a real peace based on justice and charity for all nations, especially for the small nations.

COUNCILLOR A. F. BRADBEER

(Chairman, Labour Group, Birmingham City Council):

Our immediate feelings of joy and release from tension are naturally followed by the recollection of many who have suffered and the many who will never return. Our deepest sympathy goes out to sorrowing parents, to lonely widows and fatherless children. We remember that the war still continues in the Far East. We hope that its end will come as suddenly and bring our men back safe and sound.

Modern civilisation has been shaken to its foundation. The development of international solidarity becomes a vital issue. We must learn to think and act internationally.

Our high resolve on "VE" Day must be to see that the love of our country and our gratitude for our people's bravery shall be expressed

in a ceaseless endeavour to provide them with homes and employment, and healthy, happy lives for their children.

Canon Guy Rogers asks us to say that the services at St. Martin's will be at 11.0 and 1.10 as previously announced, at 3.30 (instead of 3.0

BIRMINGHAM'S WAR-TIME STORY

"THE BIRMINGHAM POST" to-day publishes on its inside pages something of the story of the city's war-time effort. For reasons of space and paper shortage, it is neither complete nor comprehensive; and further articles covering other phases of the city's war-time activities will appear shortly.

NIGHT FLOODLIGHTING AND BONFIRES

Birmingham celebrated VE-Day to-day with spirits undamped by the rain. Street decorations soon looked bedraggled, but there was no answering gloom in the hearts of the people. The things most likely to be affected are the street bonfires planned for to-night.

After the confusion which existed yesterday, Birmingham folk settled quietly down to a break from work. There were, of course, late revellers last night in all parts of the city—and at least one licensed house went "dry." The licensee faced the prospect of celebrating VE-Day with frantic appeals to his brewery for something to sell to-night!

After a meagre showing of flags and bunting yesterday, the city streets went gay overnight. Even at midnight a "Mail" reporter caught folks putting up the decorations, while there were obvious signs from many houses that parties were in progress. There was even dancing in the streets.

Down in Bromsgrove Street, this notice caught the eye: "Please don't call for the rent; we've spent it celebrating victory."

A feature of the celebrations was the brave display made by many of the meaner suburban streets. Flags were everywhere, some authentic, many purely imaginative, and in some instances decorations which had last adorned the Christmas tree were utilised again. From house to house stretched the lines of bunting and emblems, and many a blitzed site, still scarred and ugly, was softened by a brave and somehow pathetic show.

Night Lights

The city, should the weather improve, is likely to be even gayer to-night, with lights blazing, happy crowds thronging the streets and the floodlighting of the Hall of Memory, the Cathedral and the Council House. Theatres and cinemas are expecting large crowds.

Some of the happiest homes will be those with returned prisoners of war. These boys deservedly had the time of their lives when the news broke. Neighbours feted them and gave them a hero's welcome. In those homes from which the boys have gone to the Far East there were mixed feelings. The joy of knowing one phase of the world conflict had ended was tempered with the thought that the boys in Burma are still fighting for their lives.

The west facade of the profusely decorated factory premises of Cadbury Bros. at Bournville will be floodlit to-night and to-morrow night. Dancing has been arranged at Row Heath (if wet in the Terrace Restaurant) for the employees.

The speeches of the Prime Minister and the King will be relayed to the audiences at the Odeon Cinema, New Street, this afternoon and to-night. The feature film is "Wilson," which, appropriately enough, deals with the armistice scenes nearly 27 years ago in the first world war.

A description of scenes in Victoria Square will be broadcast to-night by Godfrey Baisley from a microphone on the roof of the Town Hall. Later he will take the microphone to the Service Men's Club in Provost House. These broadcasts will be put out "live" on the home service as part of the B.B.C. VE-Day programme.

FIREWORKS AGAIN

Though there has been no public sale of fireworks for nearly six years, some long-sighted and optimistic residents had managed to save a small stock of bangers for the big day, and these were discharged last night in some districts.

LIGHT TRAFFIC

NO BUSY SCENES AT STATIONS

Many people went to work to-day, and the public transport services functioned as usual, but carrying lighter loads. Drivers and conductors demonstrated their loyalty by reporting at the garages as usual for their vehicles, but the decision was taken by the Traffic Manager to reduce the services, and many employees were sent home. Later in the day increased services will be put on.

The railways are running normal services in the Birmingham area to-day, and to-morrow Sunday services will be the rule.

"In-coming local traffics to Birmingham this morning in certain directions were very light," an official at Snow Hill said to-day. "Now we are waiting to see what happens. If we find later that we are getting a big movement of local traffic into or out of the city, we shall adjust the train services, as far as possible, to meet the altered flow of traffic during the course of the day.

"But will you please make this clear to your readers. The last trains from Birmingham to-night will be the last trains run on normal week-days, and nothing later will be put on.

Long distance traffic has also been light. There has been so far no special rush for London."

"It is very quiet on the station to-day," an official at New Street Station said. "People seem to have taken the news as a tip to stay at home."

Uncertainty Tuesday

For many workers it was uncertainty Tuesday. "The War Office has packed up, I hear, and the people have been sent back home," said one young woman bound in speculative way for a big R.A.F. dump. "Anyway, I've got my knitting with me, so I don't mind waiting if we have to go back home again." The "War Office" and the dump, of course, were both sections evacuated to "somewhere in the Midlands." One respects the censor even on VE-Day!

But factory workers seemed to have had no such qualms. Puffing leisurely through the Black Country approach (writes a "Mail" reporter) my train windows looked out on rows of little houses with the first blue smoke of newly-kindled fires only just rising from the chimneys at 8.45 a.m. Father was sitting on the back step of the kitchen waiting for the preparation of a late breakfast, and one small boy of about 12 years of age was celebrating the occasion by digging up the family shelter. Black Country chimneys were smokeless, giant cranes at rest—one with a Union Jack flying right at the top or the jib—and the roads were deserted except for a few energetic gardeners sauntering allotment-wards with spades and forks and rakes jangling together on their shoulders.

The Midland Red Bus Company operated normal services from 8 a.m. or 9 a.m. and will do so again to-morrow.

FOOD FACTS SPECIAL EDITION

FOOD SUPPLIES FOR VE-DAYS

The Ministry of Food is confident that food traders, having served the public well throughout the war years, will provide a service during the V Holiday that will enable the public to obtain their essential minimum food supplies. The Ministry makes the following suggestions to food traders and housewives:—

GROCERS should remain open on VE Day for at least one hour after the Victory announcement has been made and if possible two hours. If VE Day is a Friday grocers should open on Saturday and close on Monday, but grocers selling bread and milk should also act in accordance with the following paragraphs.

DAIRYMEN are expected to deliver milk on both VE Days just as they normally do on Good Friday or a Bank Holiday.

BAKERS should make arrangements in advance to ensure that after the announcement bread will be made and delivered to private houses and retail shops in sufficient quantities to provide at least for normal requirements. Wherever possible bakers should in addition make bread as usual for sale on VE+1 Day and on this day open their shops for one hour or possibly two hours for the sale of bread only.

Although it is expected that the public will be able to obtain bread supplies during the V Holiday housewives are advised to carry in their homes slightly more bread than usual.

SHOPS DEALING IN PERISHABLE FOODS should remain open on VE Day long enough after the official announcement to ensure that perishable goods are not wasted.

RESTAURANTS AND CAFÉS are expected to be open on both VE Days.

Every food trader is asked to display in his shop a notice telling his customers at what hours his shop will be open during the V Holiday, together with any further details useful to his customers. Retailers expecting deliveries from wholesalers on VE Day should arrange for the reception of these goods.

The Ministry of Food, London, W.1.

WINIFRED MORTON

Of the many forms of service rendered, Mrs Winifred Morton distinguished herself by providing some home comfort for young servicemen of many nations.

Mrs Morton, with her neighbour, Mrs Emily Lowe, started on their own initiative, entertaining Americans to Sunday lunch and tea. Then they read of a scheme run by a body called the Hospitality Committee.

Allied soldiers on leave from the Western Front and far from their homelands were only too happy to share life in an ordinary home for a weekend, as a break from communal residence. The Committee enrolled women willing to take men into their homes for this purpose.

A telegram would be sent to the volunteer hostess, telling her where to meet the guest or guests assigned to her. Mr and Mrs Morton had their own family, but they managed to accommodate two guests at a time at their home in Beech Street, Ladywood. The men's native countries were the U.S.A., Canada, Australia, New Zealand, Jamaica, France, Poland, Holland and Belgium.

Food rationing made things difficult, but resources were pooled and there was a party atmosphere. It was because of the warmth and cheerfulness of the hospitality at the Mortons' that word travelled back and Mrs Morton was kept busy with newcomers. She also took in our own wounded servicemen on Sundays.

At the end of the war, the Lord Mayor, Alderman Alan Giles, presented certificates to the hostesses on behalf of the Hospitality Committee, acknowledging their work.

Testimony to the lifelong gratitude of the men is the letters from them that Mrs Morton still receives.

Below: Winifred Morton stands second from the right and Emily Lowe is on the extreme right.

The King and Queen (now the Queen Mother) talking to wounded servicemen at Dudley Road Hospital, 1945.

GODFREY BASELEY:

"The BBC were putting out a hook-up programme on VJ night linking Manchester with London with Edinburgh and so on. I had been positioned on top of the Town Hall for hours. In the Square below was a bandstand which the crowd, in between dancing and singing, had turned into a bonfire. They spotted a big 'What's-on-in-Birmingham' noticeboard on the side of the

On or 'off' their machines—
DESPATCH RIDERS
SWEAR
by
KOLYNOS!
of course

For whiter, brighter teeth, 'Don R's'—the men with the blue and white sleeve bands—swear by Kolynos, in the yellow and green 'sleeve' carton. They have good reason to do so for Kolynos has a world-wide reputation as the cleansing and refreshing tooth paste. Use Kolynos twice a day and keep *your* teeth in sound and healthy condition.

Town Hall, tore it down and threw it onto the fire. At that moment my turn to broadcast came and I was able to describe the marvellous scene below.

Afterward Frank Phillips thanked me and said, 'Baseley broadcasts burning bandstand bringing brilliance to Brimingham's Bull Ring'-which may not have been geographically accurate, but it was a pretty good piece of ad-libbing."

BERTRAM YATES (Chairman of the Birmingham Savings Committee):
"During Thanksgiving week, at the end of September, 1945, we held many savings activities, with parades and an exhibition of captured German weapons, vehicles and uniforms, on the site next to the Hall of Memory. It was all very impressive and aroused a tremendous amount of interest, as did all the savings weeks held during the war years."

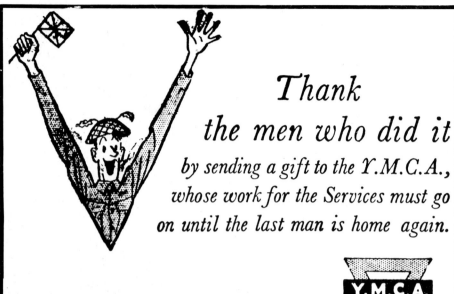
The parade held on 29th September 1945.

Crowds flocking to, and from, the exhibition of German and British militaria.

99

GERMAN
88mm ANTI-TANK GUN

A decisive weapon in the
Battle of Knightsbridge

GERMAN
Midget Submarine
BIBER CLASS
Crew: One Man. Speed 12 knots
Endurance under water: 5 hours.
Carries Two Torpedoes

GERMAN
"Human" Torpedo

The one-man "crew" sits
in special compartment
at the nose

MOBILISE YOUR MONEY

SAVED BEFORE =

JET PROPELLED
GERMAN FIGHTER AIRCRAFT
VOLKSJAGER 162

THIS AIRCRAFT HAS A MAXIMUM CEILING
OF 39,400" - A RANGE OF OVER 400 MILES
AND A SPEED AT 20,000" OF 522 MILES PER HR
ARMED WITH TWO 30m. LOW VELOCITY CANNON
THIS AIRCRAFT PROVED A FORMIDABLE WEAPON

THE SINGLE JET PROPULSION UNIT IS MOUNTED
ABOVE THE FUSELAGE.

NOTE CONSTRUCTION OF THE WING TIPS.

BIRMINGHAM'S THANKS TOTAL WAS £15,330,142

BIRMINGHAM'S Thanksgiving Week total, announced to-day, was £15,330,142. Thanking the citizens for their effort during the campaign, Mr. H. B. Yates, chairman of the Birmingham Savings Committee, said the result had exceeded original expectations, and the savers were entitled to the gratitude of the organisers in responding so well.

ALL BIRMINGHAM SAVERS = ·

EXIT

Photographs taken from German prisoners.

FACT FILE

AUGUST 1939
9 Test blackout in Birmingham
28 Evacuation rehearsals for Birmingham children

SEPTEMBER
1 Germany invades Poland with 1,500,000 troops
Italy proclaims non-belligerent status
Norway, Switzerland and Finland declare their neutrality
Evacuation of Birmingham schoolchildren begins
Blackout regulations come into force at sunset
2 Eire declares her neutrality
Further evacuations from Birmingham including mothers with very small children totalling 12,377
3 Britain and France declare war on Germany
India, Australia and New Zealand declare war on Germany
Belgium declares her neutrality
"S.S. Athenia" torpedoed and sunk without warning by a U-boat, contradicting Hitler's orders
Birmingham's first air-raid alert (a nationwide alert)
4 Advance units of BEF Land in France
10 Canada declares war on Germany
17 Russia invades Poland
27 Poland surrenders
Sir John Simon introduces our first Emergency War Budget
29 Germany and Russia formally divide Poland between them

OCTOBER
6 Hilter offers peace settlement to Britain and France
11 BEF stands at 158,000 men
12 Hitler's peace proposals rejected
14 Battleship "HMS Royal Oak" torpedoed and sunk in Scapa Flow

NOVEMBER
8 Assassination attempt on Hitler fails
30 Russia invades Finland

DECEMBER
3 Conscription in Britain extended to all males aged 19-41 and females aged 20-30 required to work as auxiliaries or on defence jobs
29 Finns defeat Russians at Suommusalmi

JANUARY 1940
5 Hore-Belisha sacked as Minister of War
8 Rationing introduced in Britain beginning with bacon, butter and sugar
Finns defeat Russians at Karelian

FEBRUARY
11 Russians launch massive attacks against Finns
17 400,000 more children evacuated from British cities

MARCH
12 Russo-Finnish war ends
29 Russia declares her neutrality in the European war

APRIL
9 Germany invades Norway and Denmark, the latter capitulating in just 4 hours

MAY
3 "HMS Aston Villa" sunk off Norway
10 Germany invades the Low Countries
Neville Chamberlain resigns as prime minister and is succeeded by Churchill
13 Germany invades France. Liège falls
14 Radio appeals by Anthony Eden for men to join Local Defence Volunteers
18 Antwerp falls to Germans
26 Evacuation of allied troops from Dunkirk begins

JUNE
9 Norway stops fighting
10 Neville Chamberlain resigns as prime minister and is succeeded by Churchill
14 Radio appeals by Anthony Eden for men to join Local Defence Volunteers
18 AntwItaly declares war on France and Britain
17 France sues for peace
night 25/26 First serious air-raid alert in Birmingham
30 Guernsey occupied by Germans

JULY
2 Hitler orders the invasion of Britain
14 Luftwaffe reconnaissance of Birmingham
19 Hitler offer peace to Britain
22 Hitler's peace proposals rejected

AUGUST
9 First bombs fall on Birmingham at Erdington
13 Birmingham subjected to a 3¹/₂ hour raid
15 Stechford area bombed
Luftwaffe launch massive attacks in an attempt to cripple the RAF
night 26/27 First major raid on Birmingham with Balsall Heath, Sparkhill and Small Heath areas hit

SEPTEMBER
7 London Blitz begins
16 Conscription introduced in USA
23 Luftwaffe reconnaissance of Birmingham
24/25 Vichy French planes bomb Gibraltar
27 Fort Dunlop hit in a daylight attack
Germany, Italy and Japan sign 10-year Tripartite Pact

OCTOBER
15 Heavy raid on Birmingham, and the first of a series that lasted for a fortnight
night 24/25 Major attack on city centre and area south of New Street station
25/26 Holloway Head and Constitution Hill bombed. A wall of fire stretching from Snow Hill to the Council House impedes the fire services. 19 people are killed when a bomb explodes in front of the screen at the Carlton Cinema, Sparkhill.
28 Italy invades Greece
29 British troops land on Crete

NOVEMBER
8 Italians suffer major defeat at hands of Greeks
11 Fleet Air Arm inflicts heavy losses on the Italian fleet at Tacanto
13 Austin aero-engine factory bombed in a daylight attack
night 14/15 Coventry devastated. Birmingham sends fire service crews to help out
19/20 Birmingham suffers a heavy raid lasting 9 hours 40 minutes. The BSA factory is badly hit with about 50 employees being killed
22 Mr. A.R. Tozer resigns as Birmingham's Chief Fire Officer
night 22/23 Worst raid on Birmingham to date. Three vital water mains destroyed, leaving much of the city without water
night 23/24 Birmingham is virtually defenceless against fire-raids. Fire appliances are moved to positions near to remaining water supplies. However there is no raid
26 8,343 children and 763 teachers evacuated from Birmingham
27 Luftwaffe reconnaissance of Birmingham

DECEMBER
night 3 4¹/₂ hour raid concentrated on Bordesley Green and Aston
by 10 Another 13,705 children evacuated from Birmingham
night 11/12 Last major raid on the city for 4 months
12 King George VI visits Birmingham

JANUARY 1941
21 "Daily Worker" closed down under Defence Regulations
22 Tobruk falls to British and Australian troops

FEBRUARY
12 German troops begin landing at Tripoli

MARCH
5 Essential Work Orders introduced
23 National Day of Prayer. Big parade of Birmingham Home Guard followed by a drumhead service arranged by the Archdeacon of Aston

APRIL
5 German troops invade Greece
night 9/10 Major raid on the east and centre of the city, Midland Arcade destroyed
night 10/11 Another heavy raid with many delayed action bombs dropped
20 Greece surrenders to Germany

MAY
10 Rudolf Hess lands in Scotland

JUNE
22 Germany invades Soviet Russia on a 1,800 mile front with 3,000,000 troops, 3,580 tanks, 1,830 planes and 600,000 vehicles
Clothes rationing introduced

AUGUST
18 National Fire Service comes into being

SEPTEMBER
2   Germans within 20 miles Leningrad

22   "Tanks for Russia" week begins in British arms factories

28   First British convoy sales for Russia

DECEMBER
1   German armour gets to within 9 miles of the Kremlin

7   Jaspanese planes attack US Pacific Fleet at Pearl Harbour

8   Britain and USA declare war on Japan

11   USA declares war on Germany and Italy

FEBRUARY 1942
15   Fall of Singapore

25   The King and Queen visit Birmingham

MAY
4-8   Battle of the Coral Sea

6   Corregidor falls to Japanese

JUNE
1   Brazilian Ambassador visits Birmingham

4-6   Battle of Midway

19   Mrs Winston Churchill visits the YMCA centre at Handsworth

21   Tobruk falls to Rommel

26   Air-raid alert for Birmingham from 1.03 a.m. to 2.29 a.m.

JULY
1   Women War Workers Bureau and Exhibition opens in Colmore Row
Churchill faces motion of censure over Tobruk

16   Air-raid alert for Birmingham 6.18 a.m. to 6.30 a.m.

23   Air-raid alert from 11.59 p.m. to 1.05 a.m.

27   Lone German aircraft fails in its attempt to bomb Solihull gas works

28   Air-raid from 1.43 a.m. to 3.39 a.m. with the west and southern parts of the city attacked and 263 fires
reported

31   Last bombs fall on Birmingham. The raid was fairly short and resulted in 41 fires

AUGUST
3   Air-raid alert from 2.57 a.m. to 3.28 a.m. and from 1.54 p.m. to 2.13 p.m.

8   Air-raid alert from 11.59 p.m. to 1.25 a.m.

12   Air-raid alert from 1.51 a.m. to 2.06 a.m.

19   Canadian and British raiding forces land at Dieppe

25   Duke of Kent killed in plane crash

SEPTEMBER
20   House to house fighting in Stalingrad

21   Lucas canteen figures issued for year ending 26th July 1942 list quantities served in Birmingham factories

Beverages	14,275,246
Breakfast	92,621
Main meals	1,489,227
Subsidiary meals	374,501
Teas	4,608,731

NOVEMBER
4   Afrika Korps defeated at El Alamein

JANUARY 1943
14   Duke and Duchess of Gloucester visit the Civil Defence Depot, Birmingham.

FEBRUARY
2   German forces at Stalingrad surrender

MARCH
13   Assassination attempt on Adolph Hitler fails

20   Second assassination attempt on Hitler fails

APRIL
23   Two bombs fall on Bordesley Green

MAY
12   Surrender of all Axis forces in North Africa

JULY
10   Allies land in Sicily

24   RAF attack Hamburg with 740 planes

25   RAF attack Essen with 627 planes

27   RAF attack Hamburg with 739 planes. 20,000 men, women and children are thought to have died in the fire storms created by incendiary bombs

SEPTEMBER
8   Italian surrender made public, though a secret armistice had been signed on the 3rd

OCTOBER
13   Itlay declares war on Germany

JANUARY 1944
14   Education Act passed

22   Allies land at Anzio

MARCH
9   General Montgomery visits Birmingham

JUNE
6   D-Day landing in Normandy

17-24   Birmingham's "Salute the Soldier" week

22   Russia launches her summer offensive on a 300 mile front

JULY
24   German troops ordered to give "Hilter salutes" for the first time

AUGUST
25   Liberation of Paris

SEPTEMBER
12   Birmingham's Fire Guard of 50,000 volunteers is stood down

DECEMBER
13   Home Guard disbanded

JANUARY 1945
1   Lloyd George made a peer

15   First Paris boat train since 1940 leaves London

FEBRUARY
12   End of Yalta Conference

MARCH
7   US troops cross Rhine at Remagen

23   British troops cross the Rhine

APRIL
1   Cheese ration cut

12   Roosevelt dies

23   Blackout ends

25   US and Soviet armies meet at the Elbe

28   Mussolini and his mistress are shot by Italian partisans

29   German forces in Italy surrender

30   Adolf Hitler commits suicide

MAY
1   Last ARP workers given a month's notice

4   German forces in North-West Europe capitulate to Montgomery

7   Unconditional surrender of German

8   VE Day

22   Rations cut again

23   Churchill resigns and forms a caretaker government

JUNE
15   Parliament dissolved

JULY
5   General Election

22   Tea ration increased to $2\frac{1}{2}$ oz. weekly

26   Result of General Election. Labour sweep to power with 393 seats

AUGUST
6   Atom bomb dropped on Hiroshima

9   Atom bomb on Nagasaki

14   Surrender of Japan

15-16   VJ celebrations in Birmingham

SEPTEMBER
1   Clothing ration reduced to 25 per cent

19   William Joyce (Lord Haw Haw) sentenced to death for treason

OCTOBER
1   Restaurant cars restored to trains (3 course lunch costs 3s 6d)

8   Ban on central heating in shops, offices and places of entertainment is lifted

23   Income tax reduced from 10s to 9s

NOVEMBER
19   Government announce plans to nationlise coal, gas and electricity

22   Nuremberg trials begin
Petrol reduced by $\frac{1}{2}$d to 1s 11d a gallon

DECEMBER
20   Labour control ends. Peolpe free to seek own jobs.

CHEERS !

ACKNOWLEDGEMENTS

(For providing anecdotes, memories, photographs, encouragement and numerous other favours)

Austin Rover, Longbridge; Barclays Bank plc; George Bartram; Godfrey Baseley; Eric Billington; Birmingham Post and Mail Staff; Birmingham Reference Library, Local Studies; Marjorie Brown; Sir Stephen Burman; CBSO; Cadbury/Schweppes Ltd.; Ron Catton; Coventry Evening Telegraph Staff; Kenneth Crisp-Jones; Alf and Ada Crowson; Joan Currier; Donald Dixon; Margaret Doggett; Fred Dorrell; Cis Fletcher; George Gould; Reg Handley; Joyce Hibbert; Leslie Hill; Bill and Betty Hodgetts; Robert Holmes; HP Foods Ltd.; IMI plc; Anne Jennings; Emily Jones; May Jones; Albert Judd; John Henry Lewis; Joan Lewis; Dorothy Lloyd; Lord Mayor's Parlour; Lucas Industries plc; Donald Lynall; Denis Martineau; Percy McGeoch; Metro-Cammell Ltd.; Midland Bank plc; Hilda Minshall; Hilda Mleczko; Winifred Morton; Harry Mulloy; Paul Nash, Imperial War Museum; Newman Tonks Ltd; Frank Oldham; PDSA; Parker, Winder and Achurch Ltd.; Douglas Preator; Victor Price; Cyril Potter; RSPCA; Rackhams; Harry Reynolds; Salvation Army; Charles Simpson; John Taylor; Thames Television Ltd.; Ray Tomkinson; WRVS; Warks. Yeomanry Old Comrades Assoc.; Harry Webb; West Midlands Police; John Whybrow; Bob Wilkes; Bertram Yates.

Please forgive any possible omissions. Every effort has been made to include all organisations and individuals involved the book.